COMPLEXITY, STAGNATION AND FRAILTY: UNDERSTANDING THE TWENTY-FIRST CENTURY

COMPLEXITY, STAGNATION AND FRAILTY:

UNDERSTANDING THE TWENTY-FIRST CENTURY

Nader Elhefnawy

TABLE OF CONTENTS

Introduction

Twenty years ago I found myself taking an increasingly deep interest in theories of history—especially those having to do with how civilizations rise and decline. The literature on the subject is, of course, old and vast, which made the stands-outs all the more striking, especially those among the newer works. Of these the one that made by far the most impression on me at the time was archaeologist Joseph Tainter's *The Collapse of Complex Societies*.

Tainter's argument was that the pattern common to the collapse of societies in the past was that their investments in complexity produced diminishing returns, which eroded their slack, and left them vulnerable to some shock that finished them off.

That statement, of course, requires a little unpacking. What, for instance, is complexity?

Well, it's a property of systems.

Okay, what are systems?

They're a set of parts or things that work together somehow. A computer or a car or a power plant is a system. A prehistoric clan or an ancient empire or a modern nation-state is a system, too.

Okay, what kind of property of those systems is complexity exactly?

Basically, it's a matter of how many things and parts are there, and the number and kinds of interconnections between them. More things and parts, more *types* of things and parts, with more and more varied connections—that makes a system more complex. When you have asymmetry, nonlinearity, synergy—when the system is more than the "sum" of its parts—you know you are looking at a more complex system. In fact, we generally measure the complexity of a system by measuring how much information it would take to run the system, describe the system, model the system, copy the system.

As far as societies go, compare a prehistoric clan of a couple of hundred people with an industrialized nation of a hundred million people. The latter has a lot more "things and parts," and a lot more organization—more institutions and subgroups and social roles. And of course it requires much more information to describe it or model it. Accordingly, whatever else you say about it, it is much, much more complex than that prehistoric clan.

Now, about those diminishing returns, and this "slack" . . .

Basically, complexity, including societal complexity, can increase in a number of ways. One is that societies become more complex as a way of solving problems. But not every problem-solving idea they implement proves to be a good one. Or what was a good idea at one point ceases to be that, or simply has unintended and troubling consequences. Or a good idea gets carried too far. The investments of resources they put into them prove bad ones, paying off less (the return, diminishing), or even leaving them with less than they put into them (the return turning negative). As resources are finite, this takes its toll, eventually eating into those spare resources they have not mobilized, which not only provide a basis for new investment, but tide them over in tough times—"buffer" them against shocks. In fact, a day may come when some new problem arises that, a little while ago, they might have had the spare resources, the slack, to handle, but for lack of those resources cannot handle that problem anymore, and the problem proves to be too much.

To cite an admittedly easy example, the Roman Empire had once been quite able not just to protect itself, but to expand, with new acquisitions providing the resources to make still new acquisitions beyond these (like captured gold hoards). However, it used up the spoils of the old conquests (like the gold), while picking up territories it cost more to defend than they were worth, while supporting the burden of an elite that got very used to being lavish when times were good, and meant to go on living that way. A significant byproduct of imperial expansion, it was by no means the only one as that wealthy elite increasingly monopolized the land and its output while avoiding or evading taxation, so that those who could pay most paid least, and those who had no choice but to pay had less and less for anyone to take in taxes. The imperial government tried to cope in various ways, but it was less and less able to work effectively—to keep order internally or protect its territory against neighbors it earlier dominated, which, of course, meant further losses in a vicious cycle that eventually proved the Empire's undoing.

I found Tainter's argument intriguing—enough so that I tried applying it to one of my areas of interest, the international security situation of today. Ultimately I developed an article out of this line of thought, arguing that modern societies were becoming more vulnerable as they grew more complex, for three reasons.

1. Advanced societies are becoming more complex, while receiving diminishing returns on that complexity, leaving them less "slack"—the "buffering capacity" that lets them cope with shocks. Abstract as it sounds, I offered a basis for measuring all these. I measured complexity through reference to the volume of information created and stored and processed and the resources committed to these tasks; and the volume of travel and trade and communication. I measured returns on the basis of the trend in the growth of Gross Domestic Product and Gross World Product. And I measured slack by way of the trend in government deficits and public and private debt. The burden of processing information and communication, the movement of people and goods, were up, making for a more complex modern civilization. However, the rate of economic growth was trending downward, suggesting falling returns on all that extra complexity. At the same time large central government

deficits were the norm and public and private debt steadily rising, implying that societies are less able to make ends meet, and so have less in the way of a buffer.

2. Advanced societies are also moving toward tighter interconnectedness—in practice, more "tightly coupled" systems, and more "scale-free networks," as our increasingly online life demonstrates. This can be a source of economic efficiency, but it also means that the points of vulnerability are more numerous, shocks at any one point having wider effects—and slack slighter.

3. The cost of security is rising due to threats like terrorism and weapons of mass destruction. In particular security was shifting away from a strategy of deterring rational actors toward a neutralization of the attacking abilities of irrational actors ready to suffer certain self-destruction for the sake of inflicting some harm. This is an intrinsically more difficult and expensive endeavor, as the technically demanding task of missile defense demonstrates. I also contended that, in line with the reorientation of thinking on this subject toward terrorism, there was an increasing burden of "hidden" security costs in the sense that while they were increasingly regarded as a national security matter, they were left out of calculations of the defense bill. Increased expenditures on emergency and law enforcement units, private security forces, and insurance rates related to such dangers, for example, not ordinarily considered when one speaks of "defense spending" (ordinarily, calculated as the formal budget of the armed forces), were all going up.

Ultimately, all this left modern societies less well-buffered than before, vulnerable at more points, and paying more for any given level of security, with the trend in all three areas in the direction of worse.

Looking back I can see more clearly than before that "Societal Complexity and Diminishing Returns in Security" was an odd paper for the security studies field, which tends to stick more closely to the traditional, "realist" theories the student learns about in International Relations 101. (Specialists specialize, after all, and alas, this does not usually broaden the horizons.) And that is without getting into all of the things that might make this specific argument unpopular. Many do not like having it pointed out that, contrary to the hype, the age of "globalization" has been an era of slowing economic growth and worsening debt burdens. They also do not like having it pointed out that so much of what has been and is being done in the name of national security is a fool's errand, worsening rather than alleviating the problem.

Somehow, though (best to leave out the names to protect the innocent, I suppose), the article ended up running in the Summer 2004 issue of the journal *International Security*.

Because it ran in that (by academic standards) high-profile publication, the article did find a number of readers over the years. Still, on the whole it does not seem that I or anyone else convinced very many in the field to consider anything like my line of argument, or look at Tainter's work, or bother with complexity theory generally. (If anything, looking at recent literature in the field I get the feeling that it is, if anything, even more fixated on old-fashioned realism than before.)

All the same, I continued thinking about the argument I made, and returning in particular to the first point discussed here—the increasing complexity of our societies and economies, and the way in which those "investments in complexity" were translating to lower returns and less slack (slower growth, more debt, etc.). Which, as a practical matter, left me writing scarcely at all about security in the narrow sense anymore, and much more about economics—producing a longer, thoroughly updated version of my analysis of the trend with regard to growth and debt, which also probes more deeply into the reasons for the difficulty than I tried to do in my first attempt at the subject. (It seemed that there were numerous connections between our sluggish, debt-loaded economic performance since the 1970s, and the neoliberal turn of that time, which I pointed out at some length. Yes, being explicitly critical of that turn this time around did not enhance my confidence in the paper's finding a home.)

In the end I wound up publishing the catchily titled "A Long-Term Trend Toward the Depletion of Fiscal-Macroeconomic Slack in the World Economy?" on my personal blog in October 2008, just as the world got an object lesson in how hyper-complexity and ultra-interconnectedness (of a type neoliberalism undeniably created) could make the system more frail while making nasty shocks to it more regular and severe occurrences.

Of course, blogs were already being marginalized in our online life in those days, social media becoming King as the attention span of the average Internet user shrank to meme-size, and I have yet to see any evidence that anyone but myself ever actually read that paper. Still, I kept thinking about the subject, returning to it time and again in succeeding years, and in 2018 polished off and published another, still longer and more exhaustively worked out version that I published via the *Social Science Research Network*, "Rising Complexity, Diminishing Returns, Shrinking Slack: Revisiting the Evidence." Alongside it I published a supplementary paper discussing the GDP estimates I used in the new paper ("Revisiting the Evidence: A Supplementary Note on GDP Estimates"), and a third item which discussed in somewhat more depth the first paper's application of my findings to the increasing discussion of the decay of the "international liberal order" ("An International System Under Stress? A Complexity Theory-Based View") that seems to me readable as the kind of strain Tainter discussed.

This volume brings this later material together. I have also included in the appendix the paper from 2008 because, while the more recent, longer paper supersedes it in many ways, its approach is different enough (not least, in its explicit attentiveness to neoliberalism) that it seems to me to offer something sufficiently different as to merit inclusion here. Altogether I hope what I suppose anyone who conducts such research hopes, that these pieces have shed some light on matters that seem to have only got more pressing since I first took an interest in Tainter's line of thought and research almost two decades ago.

-Nader Elhefnawy, August 2019

Rising Complexity, Diminishing Returns, Shrinking Slack: Revisiting the Evidence

Back in 2004 I published my article "Societal Complexity and Diminishing Returns in Security" in the journal *International Security*.[1] That article took for its starting point Joseph Tainter's theory regarding societies' tendency to "diminishing marginal returns on investments in societal complexity" making those societies more vulnerable to shock to contemporary civilization and applied it to the question of whether the world's increasing seeming complexity was making it more or less secure.[2] One of the article's conclusions was that global civilization's combination of increasingly intricate structure, slowing economic growth and mounting debt loads indicated its moving along exactly this trajectory.

Since then I had some occasion to revisit many of the relevant issues, most notably in the U.S. Army War College Quarterly *Parameters* in 2011.[3] However, I recently reexamined the data again, with the benefit of over a decade's extra hindsight, and very plausibly, a decade's further movement along this path. This

---

[1] See Nader Elhefnawy, "Societal Complexity and Diminishing Returns in Security," *International Security* 29 No.1 (Summer 2004): 153-154.

[2] Joseph Tainter, *The Collapse of Complex Societies* (New York: Cambridge University Press, 1988). Of course, complexity as such is not an end in itself. It can, in fact, be regarded as an unwanted byproduct of their strategies. Still, the term is useful because as a practical matter it is an outcome of responses like new regulations or specialized institutions for dealing with a problem.

[3] Nader Elhefnawy, "Twenty Years After the Cold War: A Strategic Survey," *Parameters* 41 No. 1 (Spring 2011): 6-17.

new paper is the result. In reconsidering the matter this paper will offer a brief overview of the essential concepts from Tainter's work and complexity theory generally, demonstrate the applicability of Tainter's theory to the international system of today, consider the data by way of this theory, and finally, consider possible courses for the amelioration of a problematic trend.

Systems, Complexity, Adaptiveness

In attempting to use Tainter's theory, it is necessary to get a firm grip on just what it means by "complex system"—with the definition of "system" a useful starting point. Simply put, systems are collections of things or parts that work together in some way. That said, systems vary in their number and variety of elements, and the interrelationships among those elements, of which complexity may be considered a measurement. The more complex a system is, the greater the number and variety of the elements and their interrelationships, a fact with significant implications.

A system of low complexity—a simple system—is likely to have clearly defined boundaries, and within those boundaries a small number and variety of parts and associated interrelationships. These relationships tend to be direct, linear and symmetrical. The system is also likely to be reasonably self-contained. This makes the system easy (simple) to describe and understand.

By contrast, a complex system is likely to have blurrier boundaries, perhaps due to its interacting significantly with other, still larger systems. Even where this is not the case it has many parts, with numerous, diverse relationships among them. Often these relationships will constitute smaller systems—sub-systems—inside of the system in question. Perhaps unsurprisingly, not only is there more going on, but aspects of that activity are likely to be nonlinear, asymmetrical, and synergistic—much more than the sum of the parts, and because the system is so sensitive to so many factors and can respond to them in so many ways, less predictable. All this makes it harder to describe and understand. In fact, the level of difficulty of describing or replicating a system's structure or workings underlies most formal measures of complexity, such that one might see complexity as a measure of "information content."[4]

Mechanical systems provide an obvious example of the difference between simplicity and complexity, with jet engines a classic example. Frank Whittle's original turbojet design had a relatively small number of parts, and only one moving part—the compressor-turbine combination. By contrast, a Boeing 747's turbofan has roughly 25,000 parts, many of them organized in elaborate sub-systems, making it a much more complex (much more information-intensive) device.

Why and how does such complexity grow? The object of increased complexity in a system is generally the improvement of that system's performance, efficiency, or resiliency. For example, the existing array of parts and relationships suggest places—niches—where new parts and relationships can usefully be added. It is even possible for whole new sub-systems to be added to the system, whether this is a matter of designing systems from scratch, or incorporating already existing systems (like a jet engine's using water injection to generate more thrust).

---

[4] Examples of such measures can be found across the range of scientific fields, from computing to biology to linguistics. See Seth L. Loyal, quoted in John Horgan, *The End of Science* (Reading, MA: Addison-Wesley, 1996), 288. This identification of commonalities within measures of complex systems does not deny the reality that a system can be complex in one way, and simple in another, Nicholas Rescher pointing out how a typewriter with a modest number of keys can produce an infinite variety of texts"—its low complexity of composition (the physical assemblage) permitting a high complexity of function (in terms of that array of texts it can produce). However, "while separable in theory, the different modes of complexity do tend to run together in practice." Nicholas Rescher, *Complexity: A Philosophical Overview* (New Brunswick, NJ: Transaction Publishers, 1998), 14-15.

Understanding Societies as Complex Systems

Human societies, whether considered at the level of unitary polities or the global system of sovereign states, can and do become more complex, and for similar reasons to jet engines. The people in them "invest" in that society's complexity, organizing its economy and associated systems more elaborately to the end of solving its problems, or improving its performance. This tends to take the shape of "more institutions, more subgroups . . . more social roles, greater specialization, and more networks . . . more vertical and horizontal controls and a greater interdependence," not least, for handling the larger information flows and heavier burden of information-processing that information-intensive complexity entails.[5]

The tendency of human societies' toward increasing complexity is such that the term "civilization" itself has long been equated with such material change and expansion, in response to imperatives ranging from demography-driven resource stress, to military and economic competition.[6] In modern times all this has

---

[5] Timothy F.H. Allen, Joseph A. Tainter and Thomas W. Hoekstra, *Supply-Side Sustainability* (New York: Columbia University Press, 2003), 62.

[6] Arnold Toynbee distinguished civilizations from other, simpler types of society by their continuous, creative response in the face of challenges, and identified as the source of their disintegration their failure to do so. For Carroll Quigley, who wrote in more concrete and materialist terms, the central feature of a civilization was its "instrument of expansion," which facilitated its demographic, economic and cultural growth in its earlier phases, but which ultimately failed to continue that expansion, plunging civilization into a crisis from which it did not usually recover. Western civilization was for him unique in its having been able to replace failed instruments of expansion twice in the past—the mercantilist capitalism of early modern times replacing feudalism, and in the eighteenth century replaced in its turn by financial capitalism. See Arnold Toynbee, *A Study of History* (New York: Oxford University, 1947); Carroll Quigley, *The Evolution of Civilizations: An*

been strongly reinforced by capitalism becoming the default mode of economic life; the enlarged use of machinery driven by inanimate power; and the deliberate pursuit of new technology sometimes referred to as "invention of invention." Altogether this resulted in an Industrial Revolution that, by way of creating the current, unprecedented societal complexity of twenty-first century global civilization, has enabled a 60-fold increase in the world's per capita economic output since 1800, and an over 400-fold increase in output overall.[7]

The Price and Perils of Complexity

While at its best permitting impressive improvements in a system's performance, the addition of more parts, more relationships and more sub-systems is not a perfect solution, whether in mechanical systems, or social ones. Creating and sustaining organization is costly, in energy as well as informational terms, while imposing limitations on flexibility at some level, as the price of being able to do *more*. All other things being equal the design, construction and maintenance of the more complex jet engine referred to earlier is costlier in comparison with its simpler predecessor.

The same goes for human societies. Contemporary civilization, despite deriving 18 times as much economic output per unit of energy as it did in 1800, consumes 27 times as much energy

Introduction to Historical Analysis (New York: Macmillan, 1961). For an exhaustive discussion of such material imperatives, see Tainter, *Collapse*, 39-90.

[7] Maddison Project Database, version 2013, last modified 11 Jan. 2018, accessed February 20, 2018, https://www.rug.nl/ggdc/historicaldevelopment/maddison/releases/ maddison-project-database-2013. J. Bolt and J. L. van Zanden, "The Maddison Project: collaborative research on historical national accounts," *The Economic History Review* 67. 3 (2014), 627–651.

overall.[8] Meeting that enlarged need has entailed the exploitation of less accessible, more costly sources, like oil deposits deep beneath the seabed, as well as mounting externalities like pollution.

The cost of that extra complexity, whether directly (like that underwater oil drilling) or through unintended "side effects" (like pollution), may eventually come to outweigh any advantages that complexity brings. This would mean diminishing returns, which are not only unfortunate in themselves but erode the system's "slack," the "buffering capacity" that enables it to withstand unexpected shocks. In the worst case there may be a negative feedback loop in which decreasing performance feeds decreasing slack and vice-versa, resulting in stagnation, dysfunction and even failure. To return to the earlier example, the redesign of a jet engine may well deliver greater fuel-efficiency, but past a certain point it will be a matter of more trouble and expense for fewer gains, with the design's difficulties outweighing the benefits of any efficiency gains. It may also be the case that making the system more efficient also makes it less reliable and robust, perhaps to the point at which it ceases to be usable.[9]

The same can happen with a society, as increasing costs and restrictions go with relatively smaller improvements in its members' well-being—diminishing marginal returns, and dwindling slack. Tainter's specific contention, in fact, is that this is the typical path

---

[8] Derived from Madison Project and "Global Primary Energy Consumption," Figure 2 in Hannah Ritchie and Max Roser, "Energy Production & Changing Energy Sources," *Our World in Data*, University of Oxford, Max Roser, accessed February 20, 2018, https://ourworldindata.org/energy-production-and-changing-energy-sources.

[9] See Elhefnawy, "Societal Complexity," 162-168. For fuller analysis of the Roman Empire from such a perspective, see Tainter, *Collapse*, 124-125, 128-152, 214-215; and Thomas Homer-Dixon, *The Upside of Down: Catastrophe, Creativity and the Renewal of Civilization* (Washington D.C.: Island Press, 2006), 235-251.

complex societies take to collapse, with the fate of the Western Roman Empire the classic example.[10] Rome's course of military-driven territorial expansion led it along a path of diminishing returns, eventually incorporating territories that were less remunerative over the longer term, due to the diminution of the prospects for importing slaves as those territories came under Roman rule; the exhaustion of farmland and forest by intensive agriculture and the associated wood consumption; and the expenditure of the gold stocks it captured when it conquered other polities (one-time gains only). As might be expected in a system dependent on slave-based agriculture, and periodic boosts from foreign treasure hoards, the result was an increasing mismatch between resources and expenses that left the Empire vulnerable to shocks (a changing climate, plague, military pressure from the foreign "barbarians"), less effective at providing essential goods (like physical security), and a heavier burden on its citizens, who were giving it more (in the form of taxes, for example) in return for less (in the form of security, for example). Increasingly they responded with evasion or even exit from the system (ceasing to be producers, or retreating into manorialism). This further undermined the Empire's resource base and fed a vicious cycle of decreasing effectiveness and increasing costs, resulting in decreasing stability, increasing susceptibility to foreign attack, territorial losses and shrinking functionality through the fourth and fifth centuries C.E., down to the point at which the Western Roman Empire collapsed outright, while the Eastern Roman Empire endured only in much modified form as Byzantium.

Those who contend that the world's current fossil fuel-based energy base is unsustainable due to the scarcity of fossil fuels, or environmental consequences like greenhouse gas emissions sometimes raise a Roman-style collapse as a possible endpoint to the present trajectory. Were such a collapse to occur it would not

---

[10] Tainter, *Collapse*, 128-152.

take quite the same shape inside a system of sovereign states as in a unitary polity. However, those states would behave in comparable ways to such a polity's members, rejecting more burdensome costs and controls and disengaging accordingly, resulting in higher conflict within the system, the system's increasing frailty, and ultimately its ceasing to exist in any meaningful sense.

Toward a Practical Application of the Concept

While Tainter's theory concerns collapse, its emphasis on the trends leading up to collapse make it useful to understanding systems suffering stress far below the level of outright collapse, including the economic, fiscal, ecological and political strains with which the world is coping today. In fact, prior work founded on Tainter's suggests the manner in which this might be done.[11]

Gauging Societal Complexity—and its Returns

As previously noted here, complex systems are by definition difficult to understand, and often defy precise quantification. Put more concretely, it is one thing to acknowledge that complexity is a measure of information content, but a very hard thing to make precise, comparable estimates of the information content of two systems, or the same system at two different points in time. Certainly there do not seem to be any time series' giving even rough estimates of the information content of human civilization as a whole for extended periods. However, if only in a fragmentary way, it is simple enough to identify those things that would be counted within a measure of information content, such as the growth of communication and trade, which are more accessible. Where the returns on investments in complexity are concerned, economic growth is a plausible if rough indicator, with markedly slowing

---

[11] Elhefnawy, "Societal Complexity," 157-162.

growth in Gross Domestic Product strongly suggestive of diminishing returns.[12]

At the same time, slack might be conceived in terms of the freedom of a society to redeploy its resources. Of course, one can construe several different kinds of slack. However, a particularly important kind is what one might call fiscal-macroeconomic, namely the economic (and especially, financial and monetary)

---

[12] Ibid. GDP is "rough" because it tends to both undercount and overcount, failing to capture costs such as the consumption of capital stock or resource depletion, while overlooking improvements not adequately reflected in market activity, like the easier access to information in the digital age. Efforts to develop more comprehensive measures, however, suggest that GDP on the whole overcounts rather than undercounts the gains, and therefore understates rather than overstates the problem. Where GDP calculations indicate as much as an 80 percent expansion in per capita income for the U.S. between 1978 and 2005, the General Progress Indicator (GPI) shows no net improvement for the country during the whole period. However, the wide use of GDP for nearly a century, and the construction of numerous lengthy time series' of the GDP of nations, regions and the world as a whole (Gross World Product) by multiple institutions and researchers; and derivative calculations of the same (regarding such matters as growth rates); are so far from being matched by any other metric that there is no practical alternative to its use. See John Talberth, Clifford Cobb and Noah Slattery, *The Genuine Progress Indicator 2006: A Tool for Sustainable Development*. Oakland, CA: Redefining Progress, 2006, accessed February 20, 2018, http://rprogress.org/publications/2007/GPI%202006.pdf. Also see Mark J. Perry, "Another Possible Limitation of GDP Accounting— It May Fail to Capture Improvements in Economic Well-Being in the Information Age," *AEIdeas* 7 May 2015, accessed February 20, 2018, https://www.aei.org/publication/another-limitation-of-gdp-accounting-it-fails-to-capture-improvements-in-economic-well-being-in-the-information-age/.

resources societies can call on in time of need to achieve a given end. One can plausibly treat public levels of spending and taxation, and public and private indebtedness (relative to output and income) as a measure of that freedom, or more precisely, the limits of that freedom. After all, taxation tends toward the tolerable maximum at a given time, while spending's exceeding revenues, and the associated deficits, imply that the resources to hand are inadequate to meet immediate needs. The consistency of such a pattern strongly suggests prolonged strain. Of course, borrowing, even when long-term, may also be a matter of long-term investment, debt amassed today for the sake of growth tomorrow. However, a long-term trend toward *relatively* higher debt suggests that if such a policy is being followed, it is not being followed successfully, with debt accumulation itself often an indicator of a frail economic performance.[13]

Taken altogether, already high levels of taxes, spending and debt (public, private and especially both) mean that much less scope to mobilize resources for new or different purposes by way of raising taxes or borrowing funds.[14] Accordingly a country where spending, taxation, deficits and debt are all rising relative to national income might reasonably be considered one with decreasing slack. (While less easily calculated, one might also identify a failure to meet established needs—for instance, deferring maintenance on or failing to protect key assets or resources, like essential elements of a nation's physical infrastructure—as another indicator of declining slack.) Furthermore, there is no reason why one cannot consider an entire international system from the standpoint of these same criteria

---

[13] The "collapse in output and asset prices . . . sap revenues and lead to higher spending through automatic stabilizers," and often associated discretionary spending, like bail-out packages for troubled institutions or supplementary spending on unemployment programs. International Monetary Fund, *Fiscal Monitor: Debt: Use it Wisely*, October 2016, 11.

[14] Elhefnawy, "Societal Complexity," 159.

of information content, growth and debt, with the pre-World War I international system an obvious example.

Example: World War I and After

The nineteenth century saw the emergence of a truly global international economic order by way of industrialization, the expansion of the Western colonial empires, and relatively free trade, underpinned by Britain and its gold-backed currency, the pound sterling. The whole world was linked together by a genuinely worldwide transport and communications network (telephone and telegraph, steamship and railroad), while international trade equaled perhaps 30 percent of the highest Gross World Product (GWP) ever generated up to that time.[15] However, as John Maynard Keynes observed at the time, this depended on an "intensely unusual, unstable, complicated, unreliable" organization of economic life.[16]

When World War I (1914-1918) broke out that organization permitted the warring states to fight on an unprecedented scale, mobilizing over 65 million soldiers, in an effort that cost some $200 billion (equal to perhaps a year's GWP at the time). However, the extraordinary depth and violence of the effort also made that war all the more disruptive. Human and physical damage aside, the economic and fiscal strain of the war saw the warring states run up not only unprecedented trade imbalances and international debts to match, but an exceedingly complex *structure* of debt that made the world's economic organization even more "unusual, unstable, complicated, unreliable " than before. The system of reparations from the Germans to the Allies, and inter-Allied debts, and the subsequent crises and fixes (like the 1923-1925 Franco-Belgian

---

[15] Mariko J. Klasing and Petros Milonis, "Quantifying the Evolution of World Trade, 1870-1949," working paper, Social Science Research Network, September 2013, accessed February 20, 2018, https://papers.ssrn.com/sol3/papers.cfm?abstract_id=2087678.

[16] This is indeed the very second sentence of his classic *The Economic Consequences of the Peace* (London: Macmillan, 1920).

occupation of the Ruhr, and the reliance of Germany on the U.S. for credit with which to pay reparations to the Allies, who paid their debts to the U.S.), exemplified this.

At the same time there was in key economies a continued adherence to policies that had outlived their usefulness, like Britain's quest to maintain the pound sterling at pre-war parity (despite Britain's transformation from international creditor to debtor). Following wartime and post-war inflation the resulting picture was of austerity, deflation and stagnation.[17] Something of an exception, the U.S. enjoyed boom times in the 1920s, but only on the basis of unbalanced trade and foreign debt that made it an international creditor for the first time, and brought a massive influx of gold into the country. The result was a massive expansion of domestic debt and speculative bubbles in real estate and stock (1925-1929), which were also connected with an increasingly complex and fragile corporate and banking structure.[18] That structure left the U.S. economy very vulnerable to the shock of a drop in asset prices, and the same went for the larger world economy of which the U.S. economy was so critical a part (the Wall Street bust causing American banks to call in their German loans, deepening that country's difficulties), resulting in a global Depression during the 1930s.

In response the major powers elevated trade barriers, devalued their currencies (Britain going off gold again in 1931, for the last time), and organized more limited economic blocs (Britain's Sterling Area, France's Gold Bloc and Germany and Japan's own regional arrangements) to protect their industries and monetary

---

[17] After the World War I boom, the British economy contracted, so that as of 1924 per capita GDP was only at its 1913 level, and in 1929, roughly where it had been in 1918. Maddison Project. For a general discussion of the relevant history, see Mark Blyth, *Austerity: The History of a Dangerous Idea* (New York: Oxford University Press, 2013).

[18] John K. Galbraith, *The Great Crash* (New York: Time Inc., 1961).

systems.[19] (They also withdrew from previous collaborative arrangements in another way, eventually acceding to the collapse of the pre-war arrangements regarding debt and reparations in the 1932 Lausanne Conference.) Retreat, however, proved no solution to the problem, the economies of the major states continuing to perform only on the basis of massive, unsustainable government interventions, like the deficit spending of the U.S., and rearmament in Britain and Germany. To the end of securing a more viable, long-term position a number of states, most notably Germany, attempted to create a larger and more self-sufficient sphere through military expansion that led to an even longer and more devastating conflict, World War II (1939-1945).

Put into Tainter's terminology, World War I subjected the international system to a massive shock, which ate deeply into the slack of its sub-systems (national economies), and the system as a whole (the overall world economy). In an attempt to preserve the system in spite of this the major sub-systems responded with new investments in complexity, with all their costs and controls at their own level, and that of the system as a whole (in their domestic fiscal and monetary policies, and the international credit and reparations arrangements). The result, however, was no return to the earlier performance, but rather continued movement along a path of diminishing marginal returns (stagnation) and receding slack (frailty) at the level of both key sub-systems (like the British and U.S. economies), and the system as a whole (the world economy). The result was that the system was increasingly vulnerable to shock,

---

[19] Klasing; Jakob B. Madsen, "Trade Barriers and the Collapse of World Trade During the Great Depression," *Southern Economic Journal* 67 No. 4 (2001): 848-868. For an analysis of the trend which presents the shift as having already been underway from before the 1929 crash, see Barry Eichengreen and Douglas A. Irwin, "Trade Blocs, Currency Blocs and the Reorientation of World Trade in the 1930s," *Journal of International Economics* 38 No.1 (February 1995): 1-24.

as demonstrated when a shock in a major sub-system (the stock market crash in the U.S.) powerfully contributed to such a degree of disruption within the overall system (the Great Depression) that its other elements increasingly substituted greater interaction within a smaller, seemingly more manageable sub-system (their currency and trading blocs) for engagement with the bigger system as a whole. The limits to such a turn led to increased conflict, which ultimately delivered another, profound shock (World War II) that completed the system's collapse.

Of course, contrary to the fears of some of the observers of the time, an industrialized, capitalist system of nation-states did endure, and even flourished, but in the form of a new system constituted out of the material of the old in what Thomas Homer-Dixon has termed "catagenesis."[20] In place of the earlier, British-led system was an American-led system, where the old laissez-faire gave way to larger and more interventionist governments, even as the United States promoted a restoration of free trade under the General Agreement on Tariffs and Trade, underpinned by institutions like the World Bank and International Monetary Fund, with regional arrangements (like the European Coal and Steel Community and its successors) generally supplementing rather than opposing the movement. Not only accompanying it but necessary for it was a moderation of great power conflict, especially at the military level, and especially in the system's "core" of advanced industrial countries. This system was consistently challenged, in the Cold War and after. However, that system prevailed through such changes as the fragmentation of the European colonial empires into a vast mass of new states in Asia and Africa; the shift of the balance of world manufacturing, general output and trade balances from the Western world to East Asia; the end of gold backing for the U.S. dollar; and the neoliberal turn in economic policymaking; and remains the international system of today.

---

[20] Homer-Dixon, *The Upside of Down*, 22.

Global Civilization After 1945: A Survey

Just as the nineteenth century international system can be considered to have faced diminishing returns on investment in complexity, dwindling slack and external shocks that precipitated its collapse by the 1940s, it is possible to look at the present-day (post-World War II) system with an eye to the same. Indeed, such a trend would be easier to find given the far greater wealth of data regarding many of the key items for particular nations and the whole world alike—measures of complexity like information content and indices of economic integration; economic growth; fiscal states; and debt.

Complexity

Just as the world's complexity in 1914 was vastly greater than what it had been a century earlier, it has grown markedly by all these measures since 1945. Indeed, given the growth in the performance of computing and communications technologies specifically designed for the sake of recording, storing, processing and transmitting information at greater than ever volumes and speeds, it seems plausible that the rate at which the world's complexity is growing has actually *accelerated*. This hypothesis would seem amply validated by the attempts to quantify humanity's stock of information itself. One of these posits that human civilization had amassed 12 exabytes of information by the late 1990s.[21] However, estimates of the "digital universe," "a measure of all the digital data created, replicated, and consumed in a single year" a short time later put the figure at 10 times that by 2005, and doubling annually toward a projected 40,000 exabytes by 2020.[22]

---

[21] Michael Lesk, "How Much Information Is There in the World?" accessed February 20, 2018, https://courses.cs.washington.edu/courses/cse590s/03au/lesk.pdf.

[22] Ranging from "banking data swiped in an ATM," to "subatomic collisions recorded by the Large Hadron Collider at CERN, transponders recording highway tolls, voice calls zipping through digital phone lines, and texting as a widespread means of

This over 3,000-fold expansion in the volume of information does not necessarily indicate a 3,000-fold expansion in the complexity of human activity, but even if a massive share of this were mere redundancy it would indicate a profound change nonetheless. Moreover, the tendency of the "digital universe" corresponds to abundant data testifying to the increasing complexity of the "economic universe." Since 1950 the volume of trade has risen more than three times as fast as Gross World Product, and Foreign Direct Investment grew faster still—sixteen times as fast after 1970. Both pieces of data suggest that each unit of output represents disproportionately more intricate economic activity, a reading supported by the rising scale and intricacy of economic entities like multi-national corporations, the turn of manufacturing to deeply internationalized "production sharing," and the outsourcing of supply and service of all kinds.

Comparable changes in the world's monetary and financial system, including the vast expansion in the size and complexity of the money supply; the trade in foreign exchange; the credit structure; and speculative activity in stock, currencies and the new products conjured out of debt (themselves complex to the point of opacity); relative to the scale of the world economy reflect and reinforce the trend.[23] Moreover, it should be noted that the interaction between

---

communications," this amounted to 130 exabytes in 2005. John Gantz and David Reinsel, "The Digital Universe in 2020: Big Data, Bigger Digital Shadows, and Biggest Growth in the Far East," *IDC Iview* December 2012, accessed February 20, 2018, https://www.emc.com/collateral/analyst-reports/idc-digital-universe-united-states.pdf.

[23] As a share of Gross World product, "broad money" rose from 50 percent of GWP in 1960 to a record 121 percent of it in 2015. World Bank, "Broad Money (% of GDP)" World Bank Open Data. Today the daily exchange of foreign currencies is reportedly in the $3-5 trillion range, making the annual trade in them 15-25 times the volume of GWP. Patrick Graham, "Daily FX Trade More Likely $3

finance and other areas of the economy has itself seen a great increase in complexity, by way of the associated intensification of merger and takeover activity; the increasing control of Non-Financial Companies (NFCs) by financial firms, geared toward maximizing the short-term asset values within that financial system; and NFCs' often opening their own financial divisions as revenue sources.[24]

Economic Growth

Of course, that leaves the question of the *return* on all of this staggering complexity growth. As it happens, the trend in economic growth in recent decades is uncontroversial.[25] The post-World War

---

Trillion Than 5—CLS," *Reuters* March 13, 2017, accessed February 20, 2018, https://www.reuters.com/article/global-forex-volumes/daily-fx-trade-more-like-3-trillion-than-5-cls-idUSL5N1GK1F5. The total value of stock traded amounted to 6 percent of GWP in 1975—but 145 percent of it in 2000, 162 percent in 2007 and a record 165 percent in 2015, a 27-fold increase. World Bank, "Stocks Traded, Total Value (% of GDP)" World Bank Open Data, accessed February 20, 2018, https://data.worldbank.org/indicator/CM.MKT.TRAD.GD.ZS?view=chart. Meanwhile, of the vastly enlarged trade in foreign currencies, where perhaps 20 percent of the activity was speculative circa 1975, today at least 80 (and perhaps over 99) percent is. Alex Andreou, "The Rise of Money Trading Has Made Our Economy All Mud and No Brick," *Guardian*, November 20, 2013, accessed February 20, 2018, https://www.theguardian.com/commentisfree/2013/nov/20/money-trading-economy-foreign-exchange-markets-economy.

[24] The U.S., where such development has been particularly evident, has seen the "FIRE" economy (Finance, Insurance, Real Estate) double its share of GDP over the latter half of the twentieth century. See Eric Janszen, *The Postcatastrophe Economy: Rebuilding America and Avoiding the Next Bubble* (New York: Penguin, 2009).

[25] According to World Trade Organization data per capita Gross

World Product (GWP) grew at the annualized rate of about 3.2 percent a year from 1950 to 1973. Between 1973 to 1995 GWP grew at about 1.3 percent a year—less than half the 1950-1973 rate. Afterward the growth rate rose to roughly 2 percent for the 1995-2008 period (2.2 percent a year 1995-2000, 1.7 percent a year 2000-2008), but then fell to 0.8 percent a year for 2008-2015, the worst performance for any seven year period in the post-World War II era. When the 1973-2008 period is taken as a whole, its rate was still just about 1.5 percent a year, less than half the earlier period's rate, and slightly under that for 1973-2015. Figures derived from Appendix A55, "World Merchandise Exports, Production and Gross Domestic Product 1950-2015," *World Trade Statistical Review, 2016,* accessed February 20, 2018, https://www.wto.org/english/res_e/statis_e/wts2016_e/wts2016_e. pdf, and adjusted using U.S. Census Bureau, International Database, accessed February 20, 2018, https://www.census.gov/data-tools/demo/idb/informationGateway.php. Maddison Project data indicates a 2.9 percent a year growth rate for 1950-1973, and then 1.8 percent for 1973-2008, with the rate running at 1 percent for 1973-1995, 2.2 percent for 1995-2000, and (anomalously) 2.9 percent a year for 2000-2008. Measuring per capita Gross World Product in constant dollars, United Nations data roughly matches the above for the latter period—1.3 percent a year growth between 1973 and 2015. Moreover, other measures may indicate the same trend in even starker fashion. The UN's current dollar-based time series on GWP, adjusted with U.S. Census population data and the U.S. Bureau of Labor Statistics Consumer Price Index inflation calculator, presents a 0.8 percent a year growth rate for the 1973-2015 period, with the growth rate actually becoming *negative* after 2008. The 1973-1995 period had 0.7 percent a year growth, then saw a spike in the 1995-2008 period to 1.7 percent a year, after which growth turned negative—a -0.8 percent a year rate for 2008-2015. See United Nations National Statistics Division, "GDP/Breakdown at Current Prices in U.S. Dollars (All Countries)," *National Accounts,* Dec. 2016, accessed October 5, 2017, https://unstats.un.org/unsd/snaama/dnllist.asp.

II period saw a historically unique period of rapid, prolonged, widespread economic growth—some 3 percent a year per capita globally for the 1950-1973 period. The rate was only a third that in the following generation (1973-1995). Growth accelerated again during the 1990s, but generally fell well short of the post-war boom, and may have been less a function of "genuine" output growth than of speculative bubbles and rising commodity prices.[26] In any event, it came to an end relatively quickly with the deepest downturn of the world economy since the Great Depression circa 2008. The decade since has been characterized by growth weak even by post-1973 standards, roughly 1 percent a year per capita or less. Indeed, at least some of the data suggests a sustained drop through this period, and even a declining trend from decade to decade since the 1960s.[27] Taken altogether, had the world economy sustained its 1950-1973 rates up to the present, per capita GWP would be twice what it is today.

This steadily weakening performance is even more apparent in a region by region examination. The downturn of the 1970s was followed by the economic crises of Latin America and Africa in the 1980s, and the economic depression in the Soviet bloc after its political collapse (1991).[28] However, it is worth noting that the

---

[26] The late 1990s saw the culmination of the American "bull market" (1982-2000), reinforced by the "dot-com bubble" (1997-2001), the bursting of which led to recession, and the loosening of lending which contributed to a housing bubble. Events in the United States had their analog in other developed nations, while developing nations in particular saw growth linked with an explosion in commodity prices during the 2000s.

[27] The WTO data shows that the 1960s saw a 3.3 percent a year growth rate, the 1970s 2.2 percent, the 1980s under 1.5 percent, the 1990s under 1.4 percent, the 2000s 1.3 percent, and the first half of the 2010s, just 1.1 percent. Derived from WTO, *World 2016*.

[28] Latin America's per capita GDP rose in the post-war boom to a new peak in 1980, contracted 8 percent by 1983, and only recovered

advanced countries accounting for a disproportionate share of global economic output, and representing the maximum extent of investments in complexity (what one might term the "complexity frontier") also saw particularly sharp drops in their own growth rates.[29] Mainland Asia was an exception to the trend, but its more advanced economies suffered nonetheless, as did the region more broadly, with even the principal driver of growth in the twenty-first century, China, seeing a noticeable slowdown while still well short of the income level of the developed countries from 2012 on.[30]

---

its earlier level in 1994. The subsequent two decades saw a mere 1.4 percent a year rate of growth, which leaves its growth for the period at 0.9 percent. Africa stagnated earlier, but hit its 20th century peak at the same time, suffered a more severe contraction (falling 11 percent below that level by 1994), and did not recover its earlier level until 2003. Its record is 0.7 percent a year 1980-2015, and 0.6 percent a year for 1976-2015. Russia's per capita GDP collapsed 40 percent between 1990 and 1996. Calculated from UN data. See United Nations National Statistics Division, "Per Capita GDP at Constant 2005 Prices in U.S. Dollars (All Countries)," *National Accounts*, Dec. 2016, accessed October 5, 2017, https://unstats.un.org/unsd/snaama/dnllist.asp.

[29] In 1950-1973, the per capita growth rate of the U.S. was 2.5 percent, Western Europe 4 percent, Japan 8 percent. By contrast in 1973-2008, it was under 2 percent for all concerned. A continued drop was also apparent here, if after remaining on a lower plateau for a period. Europe saw its rate drop from 3.8 percent in the 1960s, to 2.5 percent in the 1970s, 1.8 percent in the 1980s and 1990s, and 0.8 percent in the 2000s; Japan from 8.4 percent in the 1960s to 3.3-3.4 percent in the 1970s and 1980s, but then 0.9 percent in the 1990s, and 0.6 percent in the 2000s. The drop was less steady in the case of the U.S., but growth still fell from 2.9 percent a year in the 1960s to 2.1-2.2 percent between the 1970s and 1990s, and then to 0.6 percent in the 2000s. Derived from Maddison Project Data.

[30] The Japanese slowdown apart, South Korea, which clocked an impressive 7.6 percent a year per capita growth rate in 1973-1997,

Consequently, the surge of complexity, and in particular of international trade, investment and financial activity, has correlated very strongly with a pronounced drop in growth.[31]

Fiscal States and Debt

The post-World War II era was, from the start, characterized by larger states, and after the conflict, massive central government debts. Little in the way of detailed, comprehensive data regarding the global picture is available, but a good deal is available on the advanced states. These generally saw a tendency toward small deficits and a dramatic contraction in debt-to-GDP ratios during the post-World War II generation, largely due to rapid economic growth that filled government coffers, and broadened the base on which old debts rested.[32] However, from the 1970s on the trend inverted, with

---

saw its rate nearly halve after the Asian financial crisis to 4 percent in 1997-2008, and then drop again to 2.6 percent for 2008-2015— all while still well under the income level of the G-7 countries. Between 1978 and 2012 China managed an 8.8 percent a year growth rate. However, this subsequently fell from year to year, to 7.2 percent in 2013, 6.8 percent in 2014, and 6.3 percent in 2015. Calculated from UN data, "Per Capita GDP at Constant."

[31] Relative to GWP trade grew at the rate of 1 percent a year in the 1960-1972 period, but this accelerated to 2.6 percent a year in 1991-2008. Derived from World Bank, "Trade." Foreign investment grew at a rate of 9 percent a year in 1970-1990, but over 14 percent a year in 1990-2007. From World Bank, "Foreign Direct Investment," adjusted for inflation using the BLS CPI inflation calculator.

[32] The U.S. is an obvious and critical example. U.S. Federal government outlays rose 60 percent relative to GDP (from 11.3 to 18.1 percent) between 1948 and 1973, a growth that was much more rapid than that of the rate of taxation (15.8 to 17 percent). However, thanks to the rapidity of economic growth in this period, the U.S. ran budget deficits of 2 percent of GDP or over in only 5 of these years, and a deficit of 3 percent only once (3.1 percent in 1968, at the Vietnam War's height). As a result the Federal debt-to-GDP ratio

economies growing more slowly, tax revenues suffering, deficits growing and debt accumulating over time. Over the subsequent four decades this combination of trends meant that in the Group of Seven advanced industrial nations gross central government debt tripled and net debt quadrupled relative to their GDP.[33] This has left five of the seven with net liabilities exceeding a year's GDP, and the two

---

fell from 119 percent to under 33 percent. By contrast, U.S. Federal outlays tended to the 19-22 percent of GDP range since then (within this range in 29 of the 42 years of the 1975-2016 period), with the periods of greater spending confined to the early 1980s hike in military spending (1982, 1983, 1985) and the aftermath of the 2008 crisis (2009-2012). (The principal exceptions were 1976-1981, when rapid inflation reduced the debt-to-GDP ratio to 31.7 percent; and 1995-2001, when the combination of stringent budget-cutting and growth exceptional for the post-1973 period again constrained and then lowered the load.) Despite this relative restraint the U.S. ran budget deficits over 2 percent in 37 of these 42 years, and budget deficits of 3 percent or over in 29 years, these once exceptional circumstances now the norm. Budget deficits of 4 percent or over, unseen in the 1947-1973 period, occurred in 15 years, deficits of 5 percent or more in 9 years, with the peak figure 10.8 percent in 2009 at the height of the recent financial crisis. As a result the Federal debt-to-GDP ratio is returning to its post-World War II level (already 106 percent in 2016). Data derived from Office of Management and Budget, "Summary of Receipts, Outlays and Surpluses or Deficits as Percentages of GDP, 1930-2023," *Historical Tables*, White House, accessed February 20, 2018, https://www.whitehouse.gov/omb/historical-tables/.

[33] Central government gross liabilities were 42.8 percent of GDP in 1973, and 125.8 percent of GDP by 2014. Net debt rose from 22.8 percent of GDP, to 86.8 percent of the figure. . *Fiscal Reference Tables*, Department of Finance, Canada, September 2015, accessed February 20, 2018, https://www.fin.gc.ca/frt-trf/2015/frt-trf-15-eng.asp.

exceptions (Canada and Germany) not much short of that.[34] Similarly China's debt has more than doubled relative to its GDP (representing another sixth of the world total) between 1997 and 2016, in spite of the exceptional, five-fold growth of its economy over this time frame.[35] Meanwhile, lower (state, provincial, local) levels of government have also seen their own debt burdens rise, if at a less spectacular pace.[36] Indeed, altogether public debt is in the range of $60 trillion worldwide today, equal to roughly 80 percent of GWP when measured at official exchange rates.[37]

Additionally, while less publicized, private sector debt has been similarly fast-growing in this time frame, and considerably larger than at least official public debt—perhaps as much as seventy percent larger by volume.[38] All of this implies a picture of a

---

[34] The 2014 net liability figures for Canada and Germany were 94.8 percent and 82.3 percent, respectively. Ibid.

[35] International Monetary Fund, "General Government Gross Debt for China," Federal Reserve Bank of St. Louis, December 13, 2017, accessed February 20, 2018, https://fred.stlouisfed.org/series/GGGDTACNA188N.

[36] In the United States state and local government debt (excluding employee retirement funds) were already 13 percent of U.S. GDP in 1973, and rose to over 20 percent by 2011. Board of Governors of the Federal Reserve System, "State and Local Governments, Excluding Employee Retirement Funds; Credit Market Instruments, Liability Level," Federal Reserve Bank of St. Louis, December 7, 2017, accessed February 20, 2018, https://fred.stlouisfed.org/series/SLGSDODNS. While below its recent peak at $3 trillion, it still amounts to an additional 2-4 percent of GWP, depending on the measure.

[37] See IMF, *Debt*. The figure is also publicly available on the debt clock posted online by the *Economist* magazine.

[38] The private debt figure was under half of GWP in 1960, then 64.3 percent in 1977, but doubled over the next two decades to hit a record level of 135 percent (1999). Since that time it has not fallen below a still-high 117 percent (in 2011). Since then it has resurged

prolonged, rapid rise of debt relative to income of all types and all levels, and this globally, as indicated in a rare attempt at a truly worldwide inventory by the International Monetary Fund in October 2016. Examining 113 countries accounting for an estimated 94 percent of world economic activity, it calculated the level of world debt at $152 billion, or some 225 percent of Gross World Product.[39] In line with the reality that in examining a complex system critical sub-systems warrant their own, special attention, it is worth noting the condition of the three largest and most influential national economies, namely those of the United States, China and Japan, which are especially worrisome from this standpoint. The U.S., which may have seen its credit-to-GDP ratio quadruple between 1964 and 2007, now has a combined public-private debt load equal to 370 percent of its GDP, while China's is also over 300 percent.[40]

---

toward a new record (at 131.6 percent in 2016). World Bank, "Domestic Credit to Private Sector (% of GDP)," World Bank Open Data, accessed February 20, 2018, https://data.worldbank.org/indicator/FS.AST.PRVT.GD.ZS.

Adjusted for inflation, U.S. corporate debt more than doubled relative to GDP, from 15 to 32 percent of the figure between 1973 and 2016. Board of Governors of the Federal Reserve System, "Nonfinancial Corporate Business; Debt Securities; Liability, Level," Federal Reserve Bank of St. Louis, December 7, 2017, accessed February 20, 2018, https://fred.stlouisfed.org/series/NCBDBIQ027S.

[39] International Monetary Fund, *Fiscal Monitor*, 19.

[40] John Mauldin, "U.S. Nonfinancial Debt Rises 3.5 Times Higher Than GDP," *Forbes* April 18, 2016, accessed February 20, 2018, https://www.forbes.com/sites/johnmauldin/2016/04/18/us-nonfinancial-debt-rises-3-5-times-higher-than-gdp/#2b07ca427f40; Silvia Amaro, "China's Debt Surpasses 300 Percent of GDP IIF Says, Raising Doubts Over Yellen's Crisis Remarks," June 28, 2017, accessed February 20, 2018, https://www.cnbc.com/2017/06/28/chinas-debt-surpasses-300-

While Japan's economy is smaller in size, its total private and public debt load is even heavier—some 600 percent of its GDP.[41]

As if all this were not enough, it should be remembered that even this dramatic indication of a trend toward greater indebtedness may yet underrepresent the actual level of strain due to the fact that that the common methods of calculating national deficits and debts, let alone global figures, do not take full account of government liabilities. Far and away the most obvious factor left out is pension liabilities, which are unaccounted for in the more comprehensive figures cited above. However, this can also be a matter of concealing, deferring or shifting costs in other ways, like cutting back on goods previously deemed essential, with underinvestment in a nation's physical infrastructure an obvious example.[42]

All of this suggests that a more rigorous accounting method would show still higher strain, which is all the more striking because of the changed political context. In the 1948-1973 period, the major governments were ideologically committed to economic regulation for a host of ends, and stronger public services and social safety nets, all to be paid for with progressive taxation. By contrast, the post-

---

percent-of-gdp-iif-says-raising-doubts-over-yellens-crisis-remarks.html.

[41] Narayanan Somasundaram and Benjamin Purvis, "Pimco's Baz Says Japan's In a Bind as Total Debt Tops 600 Percent of GDP," *Bloomberg Markets*, August 30, 2016, accessed February 20, 2018, https://www.bloomberg.com/news/articles/2016-08-30/pimco-s-baz-says-japan-in-a-bind-as-total-debt-tops-600-of-gdp.

[42] The neglect of U.S. infrastructure is a recurring theme of American politics, consistently highlighted by the American Society of Civil Engineers' annual Infrastructure Report Card, which estimates the price of remedying the neglect as $2 trillion—over 10 percent of U.S. GDP. For the current edition, see ASCE Committee on America's Infrastructure, *2017 Infrastructure Report Card: A Comprehensive Assessment of America's Infrastructure*, accessed February 20, 2018, https://www.infrastructurereportcard.org/wp-content/uploads/2017/10/Full-2017-Report-Card-FINAL.pdf.

1973 explosion of debt came under neoliberal-minded governments explicitly committed to cutting spending, deficits and debt, which eroded or eliminated much of that earlier regulatory and welfare structure. All of this can be taken as testifying not only to decreasing slack within the international economic system, but to the use of credit as a driver of growth paying diminishing returns as an economic strategy.[43]

Explaining the Trend

Establishing that human civilization has both grown much more complex (as indicated by the information burden), and at the same time seen diminishing returns and decreasing slack as a result (stagnating economic growth, fiscal strain, increasing indebtedness), merely draws a correlation. It does not necessarily demonstrate a clear cause-and-effect relationship between one and the other. Put more simply, one has to consider *how* investments in complexity led to slowing growth, mounting debt and their associated problems.

Understanding the trend toward requires at least some attention not just to the years of slowing growth, but the years that preceded them—the years of the post-war boom. The period saw a remarkable burst of growth in economic productivity, which seems traceable to a number of major developments around the middle of the century, particularly in the United States.[44] Already the country

---

[43] Writing of the United States Richard Duncan observed that between "1952 to 1968, credit grew by 5 percent a year, while the GDP grew by 3.9 percent, a gap of 1.1 percentage points." However, as credit grew more quickly, while GDP growth slowed, the gap rose to 1.9 percent a year for 1968-2007, and in 1981-2007, 2.6 percentage points a year. Richard Duncan, *The New Depression: The Breakdown of the Paper Money Economy* (Hoboken, NJ: John Wiley & Sons, 2012), 88.

[44] Annualized growth rates of output per head were 2.8 percent a year in 1920-1970, versus 1.6 percent a year for 1970-2014. The

pioneering "Fordist" mass manufacturing, giving it twice the worker productivity of other advanced industrial powers like Britain or Germany, World War II saw its economy consolidated into a smaller number of more productive units, massive government-funded capital investment in new plant and the pressure of a years-long all-out production effort with its opportunities for "learning by doing."[45] All of this translated to massive capital deepening and opportunity for improvements in American manufacturers' Total Factor Productivity, pushing the world's "productivity" frontier that much further outward.[46]Afterward the high levels of early Cold War defense spending by the United States continued that push in lesser degree, and more generally stimulated the U.S. economy. It also encouraged ongoing social trends toward women's increased participation in the work force, and more generally, higher

---

disparity in Total Factor Productivity was even greater, TFP grew at an annualized rate of 1.9 percent a year during the 1920-1970 period, fell to under 0.6 percent, and after a brief burst around the turn of the century, fell lower still to 0.4 percent in 2004-2014. See Robert J. Gordon, *The Rise and Fall of American Growth: The U.S. Standard of Living Since the Civil War* (Princeton, NJ: Princeton University Press, 2016), 17, 575.

[45] Measured by value the U.S. industrial base expanded by about sixty percent in the 1940-1944 period ($25 billion built, in comparison with a $40 billion national plant earlier), an effort which, by adding so much new plant, also represented a great updating of the whole. The Federal Treasury directly paid the bill for two-thirds of the plant, while indirectly covering the rest through "accelerated amortization" under "certificates of necessity." See J.A. Krug, *Wartime Production Achievements and the Reconversion Outlook*, Report of the Chairman, War Production Board, 9 Oct. 1945. The U.S. stock of machine tools doubled between 1942 and 1945. Gordon, *Rise and Fall*, 553.

[46] Total Factor Productivity grew at 3 percent a year during the decade of the 1940s when taken as a whole. Gordon, *Rise and Fall*, 548-553.

education, producing a work force that was both much larger and more skilled.

Given that the U.S. economy accounted for nearly half the world total circa 1945, this was in itself enough to significantly boost worldwide growth. However, it is notable that many major economies, particularly those of Germany and Japan, also underwent massive wartime capital investment and economic modernization more generally, much of which survived the damage of the war.[47] The major economies of Europe and Asia, moreover, benefited from more direct American stimulus (U.S. aid and military spending circulating dollars in these economies). Meanwhile, as these regions rebuilt, they not only counted the resumption of pre-war income levels as "growth," but played catch-up to the American model so far out ahead.[48] And that expansion, by enabling them to

---

[47] For Germany, see Barry Eichengreen and Albert Ritschel, *Understanding West German Economic Growth in the 1950s*, Working paper No. 113/08, December 2008, 8; Werner Abelshauser, "Germany: Guns, Butter and Economic Miracles." In ed., Mark Harrison, *The Economics of World War II: Six Great Powers in International Comparison* (New York: Cambridge University Press, 2000), 122-176. For Japan, see Akira Hara, "Japan: Guns Before Rice." In Mark Harrison, ed., *The Economics of World War II*, Table 6.14, 264; Alan S. Milward, *War, Economy and Society, 1939-1945* (Berkley: University of California Press, 1977), 86, 188; Bernd Martin, *Japan and Germany in the Modern World* (New York: Berghahn Books, 1995).

[48] It might be added that a portion of what looked like "growth" in this period was actually the return of GDP to earlier levels. GWP in 1950 was almost 4 percent below its 1940 level, with the regression more apparent in certain key countries. Germany took until 1955 simply to return to its 1939 level of per capita output, Japan until 1956 to return to where it had been in 1940. On the whole Europe and Japan raised their per capita GDPs from half the U.S. level to three quarters of it between 1950 and 1973. See Maddison Project.

pay for the imports that the U.S. was virtually alone in being able to provide, redounded yet again to the benefit of the United States.

By the 1970s all of this was running its course, not least because of the changed position of the United States. The extraordinary U.S. share of world output in the 1940s was an exceptional, temporary situation virtually bound to vanish amid the very recovery and catch-up of other states that did so much to fuel American growth, and indeed, by the early 1970s the American share of GWP was down to under a third. Additionally, where it had a wide open field for its exports, American industry now faced a more "level playing field," and increasingly intense competition on it. Along with the prolonging of the Cold War and its economic demands, and those demands' spiking with two major "hot" wars in as many decades (Korea and Southeast Asia), this made early Cold War levels of defense spending unsustainable for its economy generally, and its balance of payments particularly. Ultimately American policymakers terminated the gold standard, and even the more "hawkish" U.S. governments that followed tempered their defense spending accordingly, which never again reached 1950s-era levels as a share of Gross Domestic Product.[49] Additionally, the enlargement of women's participation in the work force, and the universalization of higher education, had largely been carried through, and so in and of themselves were producing fewer gains.[50]

---

[49] During the Reagan administration defense spending as a share of GDP peaked at 6.2 percent in 1985-1986, a level markedly lower than in any single year of the 1951-1972 period. The 1952-1962 years did not see a single year's spending drop below the 9 percent level, the 1952-1964 period a year below the 8 percent level, the 1951-1971 period a single year below the 7 percent level. *Historical Tables*.

[50] Women's labor force participation rose from 32.7 percent in 1948 to 44.7 percent in 1973—a 1.25 percent a year growth rate. The rate slowed afterward, to 1.15 percent for 1973-1999, when it peaked at 60 percent, but has since dropped—along with the male labor force

This combination of reduced GDP size, and strain amid a protracted defense effort and renewed competition, meant the U.S. was less able to drive global growth than before even had it made the same efforts, while Europe and Japan's completion of their rebuilding and catch-up process largely exhausted that source of gains.

In short, the post-World War II international system was heavily dependent on the exploitation of the possibilities of Fordist mass manufacturing; the enlargement and upskilling of labor forces; and American government-provided stimulus to its own economy, a key sub-system of the whole, which moved the larger system

---

participation rate. "Employment Status of the Civilian Noninstitutional Population, 16 Years and Older, by Gender, 1948-2014 Annual Averages," Table 2, "Women in the Labor Force: A Databook," *BLS Reports*, December 2015. The same goes for educational attainment. The percentage of adults 25 or older with a high school diploma or higher went from under 25 to almost 60 percent of the population between 1940 and 1973—expanding at a rate of over 2.7 percent a year. Afterward the rate was 2 percent for the rest of the 1970s, 1.2 percent in the 1980s, 0.8 percent in the 1990s, and under 0.4 percent 2000-2016 (so that it now sits at 89.1 percent). Simply put, there was a decreasing proportion of women outside the labor force, and adults without high school diplomas. There may have similarly been a trend toward diminishing returns on the expansion of college education. The percentage of adults with a bachelor's degree or higher rose 3.1 percent in the 1940-1973 period (rom 4.6 to 12.6 percent). This actually rose in the 1970s (to 4.4 percent for the rest of the decade), but slipped to 2.3 percent in the 1980s, 1.9 percent in the 1990s, and 1.7 percent for the 2000-2016 period. Derived from Table A-2, "Percent of People 25 and Over Who Have Completed High School or College by Race, Hispanic Origin and Sex: Selected Years 1940 to 2016," Educational Attainment in the United States, United States Census Bureau, 31 Mar. 2017. Consequently, while less striking than the slowed rate of growth in Total Factor Productivity, the contribution of education to rising output also slowed. Gordon, *Rise and Fall*, 17.

forward directly as well as through emulation. And by the 1970s investment in complexity in all of these areas (the exploitation of Fordist technique, additional years of education, the economic boost of U.S. defense spending) yielded fewer returns than before (the U.S. economy, certainly, under mounting strain as a result of its past efforts, which did less for the system as a whole as it continued to expand).

In hindsight, it can easily appear that the viability of the system in such ways as growth expectations and fiscal policies rested on these exhaustible sources of development (much as the Roman Empire depended on finite opportunities for territorial expansion and exploitation), and that it became less viable after those sources' exhaustion. However, it is not necessarily the case that this fully accounts for the change. Indeed, many an observer has pointed to still other factors, most commonly three areas of investments to diminishing marginal returns, namely technology, natural resources and the role of finance.

Technological Stagnation

The claim that technological research and development may be stagnating flies in the face of the conventional wisdom. However, this is arguably because of the narrow sense in which the term "technology" is used—as a synonym for digital computing and communications, to the exclusion of all the rest of technology. Numerous observers have noted that outside that area, progress has been less striking, especially in such hugely consequential fields as transport, construction, sanitation, the production of food and energy, and medicine. Indeed, some of these areas have seen a conspicuous *slowing* of progress, with analysts of medical research coining the term "Eroom's Law" (Moore's Law in reverse) to refer to the rising cost of drug discovery. Moreover, contrary to popular perceptions, computers' contribution to productivity improvement have disappointed many observers, Robert Solow famously writing of a "productivity paradox" in the late 1980s.[51]

Economic observers have offered an abundance of explanations for this seemingly counterintuitive situation. Robert Gordon cites the fact that, just as the World War II productivity explosion or the transformation of the labor force were unrepeatable boosts to economic output, so were many of the technologies of the late nineteenth and twentieth centuries, such as the incandescent light bulb. By using electricity to make light available "at the flick of a switch," the light bulb "extended day into night," revolutionizing economic life in many ways, as by making 24-hour manufacturing a possibility. New lighting technologies may confer real economic advantages, like the greater energy-efficiency of Light-Emitting Diodes, but the consequences are slighter than the advent of electric lighting as such.[52]

Gordon has made a similar case regarding information technology. As he observes, Internet content and usage has tended to involve "preexisting forms of information," often as a duplicate of old media still in production, rather than supplying fundamentally new goods and services, with the replacement or simply supplementing of brick-and-mortar stores with online retail an obvious example—a fairly obvious example of greater complexity, without commensurate return from the standpoint of economic

---

[51] Robert M. Solow, "We'd Better Watch Out: Review of *Manufacturing Matters*," *New York Times*, July 12 1987, 36. With the benefit of longer hindsight, Robert Gordon has identified an impressive burst of growth in the 1996-2004 period, but that progress returned to the norm afterward. Gordon, *Rise and Fall*, 17.
[52] Robert J. Gordon, "Does the New Economy Measure Up to the Great Inventions of the Past?" National Bureau of Economic Research Working Paper 7833 (Aug. 2000); Robert J. Gordon, "Does the 'New Economy' Measure Up to the Great Inventions of the Past?" *Journal of Economic Perspectives* 14 No. 1 (Fall 2000): 72.

life.[53] Gordon also points to a second aspect of the use of computers in economic life, namely the limited extent to which computers and computer-controlled machinery have been substitutable for humans in activities requiring responses finely individualized to the detailed demands of specific situations, especially where this also entails eye-hand coordination.[54]

Another, even more deeply rooted, possibility is that scientific research itself may be an area of diminishing returns. One suggestion is that the sheer mass of information already amassed, and continuing to be amassed, is overtaxing the ability of researchers to generate genuine *knowledge* from it.[55] This has arguably been reflected in such concrete ways as the increasingly specialized and collaborative character of scientific work (evidenced in the ever-growing coauthoring of papers), and the more advanced ages at which scientists make significant contributions than in prior generations, suggesting that more man-hours of training and research must go into any discovery.[56]

---

[53] Gordon, "Does" (Aug. 2000), 70.

[54] Gordon, "Does" (Aug. 2000), 65.

[55] Nicholas Rescher has written of the "law of logarithmic returns": "As information proliferates, we confront a situation of redundancy and diminished productiveness. Any knowable fact is always surrounded by a vast penumbral cloud of relevant information . . . really significant facts become more difficult to discern." Rescher, 78. For the fuller discussion, see Rescher, 77-90.

[56] The tendency toward greater specialization would seem underlined by the fact that the age at which researchers make their major contributions is rising. Zoe Corbyn, "Experience Counts for Nobel Laureates," *Nature News*, November 9, 2011, accessed February 20, 2018, https://www.nature.com/news/2011/111107/full/news.2011.632.ht ml. "Pick any recent issue of *Science* and count the number of authors per paper," Allen and his coauthors challenge the reader. Allen et. al., *Supply-Side*, 89.

Natural Resource Depletion and Ecological Disruption

In addition to the stagnation of technological progress in many critical areas, the world economy is coping with prolonged and deepening resource stress. The current estimate is that it consumes the resources of "1.6 Earth equivalents"—a significant margin of overshoot, which cannot but raise resource costs.[57] A full discussion of the problem is beyond the scope of this article, but some attention still seems due the problems raised by fossil fuels because of their special role within the world's energy-transport system, and the scale of their contribution to the largest single environmental problem of today, anthropogenic global warming.

To be sure, the price of the fuels has fluctuated over time. However, while at best ambiguously reflected in market prices, the ever-more intensive production of energy from fossil fuels (seen in enlarged output dependent on costly and difficult supplies like offshore fields and tar sands) has consistently yielded diminishing returns, as evidenced in the falls in Energy Return On Energy Invested (EROEI) and the rate of discovery of new supplies.[58] All this is without taking into consideration the significant "hidden"

---

[57] The widely-cited figure comes from the Global Footprint Network, accessed February 20, 2018, https://www.footprintnetwork.org/. Assuming the 1950-1973 growth rate had continued at a comparable resource intensity, we would therefore be using three Earths now, an implausible combination suggestive of the ways in which environmental constraints have undermined growth.

[58] See Nader Elhefnawy, "The Impending Oil Shock," *Survival* 50 No. 2 (Apr.-May 2008): 37-66. In the absence of a widely agreed-upon methodology for performing such calculations, different analysts arrive at such varying EROEI figures that at a glance they can appear to evidentiate any claim. However, the calculations generally demonstrate the dropping return on investment as these more difficult sources are utilized. See Charles A.S. Hall, Jessica G. Lambert and Stephen B. Balogh, "EROI of Different Fuels and the Implications for Society," *Energy Policy* 64 (Jan. 2014): 141-152.

costs of these resources—both subsidies (including the subsidy of military spending aimed at protecting access to oil supplies), and externalized but mounting costs like pollution, increasingly apparent as the effects of global warming are better understood, more easily recognized and increasingly severe. Estimates of these costs vary greatly, but a recent International Monetary Fund study put the total at 6 percent of GWP and growing, while a still higher estimate is quite plausible given that the study took no account of the costs of resource conflict, or the opportunity costs of forgoing alternative uses for these resources.[59] All of this is quite ample to depress the long-term rate of economic growth, which has plausibly been a register of these problems.

Financialization

As noted earlier, the rising integration of the world economy has been strongly accompanied by larger and more intricate volumes of trade, financial activity and credit, which has not been seen as a positive or even neutral development by all observers. Indeed, the ownership of NFCs by financial firms has been blamed by many for encouraging a preoccupation with short-term asset values, and with speculation generally, at the expense of productive material investment. Even where the non-financial activity of the NFCs is concerned, this may have had implications ranging from the diminution of the intensity of technological research and development, to the purchase of the short-term efficiency of their operations at the expense of their resilience.[60] In certain cases, this

---

[59] David Coady, Ian Perry, Louis Sears and Baoping Shang, "How Large are Global Energy Subsidies?" working paper, *International Monetary Fund*, May 2015, 5-6.

[60] For discussions of short-termism, see Angela Black and Patricia Fraser, "Stock market short-termism-an international perspective," *Journal of Multinational Financial Management* 12 No.2 (April 2002): 135-158; James Crotty, "The Neoliberal Paradox: The Impact of Destructive Product Market Competition

practice by single sectors may have been sufficient to undermine the performance of whole economies (like electric companies saving money at the expense of grid reliability).[61] Additionally, to the extent that this approach has enabled once unimaginable trade balances to accumulate; and made speculation more intense, more complex and less well-regulated; it has been associated with more frequent and severe financial crises.[62] This may be said to have undermined the long-term growth trend yet again, while through the explosion in government deficits and debt loads, eating deeply into

---

and Impatient Finance on Nonfinancial Corporations in the Neoliberal Era," Policy Economic Research Institute, Research Brief (Jul. 2003); Crotty, "The Neoliberal Paradox: The Impact of Destructive Product Market Competition and 'Modern' Financial Markets on Nonfinancial Corporations in the Neoliberal Era," in ed. Gerald Epstein, *Financialization and the World Economy* (Cheltenham, UK: Edward Elger, 2005), 77-107; John R. Graham, Campbell R. Harvey, and Shivaram Rajgopal, "The Economic Implications of Corporate Financial Reporting," *Journal of Accounting and Economics* 40 (2005): 3–73.

[61] One assessment is that grid unreliability cost the U.S. economy $120 billion in 2001 alone. George F. McClure, "Electric Power Transmission Reliability Not Keeping Pace with Conservation Efforts," *Today's Engineer Online*, Feb. 2005. Accessed February 20, 2018, http://te.ieeeusa.org/2005/Feb/reliability.asp.

[62] For a discussion of the link between trade balances and speculative bubbles, see Richard Duncan, *The Dollar Crisis: Causes, Consequences and Cures* (Singapore: John Wiley and Sons, 2003). Between 2007 and 2012 the central governments of the G-7 nations took on additional liabilities equivalent to about two-fifths of their economic output, raising their gross debt-to-GDP ratio 50 percent (from 81.7 to 123.3 percent), and their net debt-to-GDP ratio an even more staggering 73 percent (from 49.7 to 85.3 percent). *Fiscal Reference Tables*, Department of Finance, Canada, September 2015, accessed February 20, 2018, https://www.fin.gc.ca/frt-trf/2015/frt-trf-15-eng.asp.

countries' slack (with the sharp enlargement of deficits and debt loads in the wake of 2008 a case in point).[63]

Defenders of the trend toward financial complexity and its greater prominence in economic life argue for the importance of a large, dynamic (and lightly regulated) financial sector for all that, insisting that without it such economic growth and technological progress as has been seen since that time (e.g. the "digital revolution") would have been impossible. However, taking this as the best possible outcome affirms rather than refutes the picture of a system delivering diminishing returns, even as credit and financial innovation themselves seem to pay diminishing returns as a growth strategy.

What Next?

The current combination of rising complexity and diminishing returns on it, today well advanced, may also be increasingly worrisome, with slowing growth, debt burdens, and the violence of economic and other shocks arguably translating to an increasing frequency and severity of international crisis amid the "Great Recession," the European Union's sovereign debt crisis, and the deteriorating relations between Russia and China with their neighbors and the West. Already comparisons of present-day troubles with those of the 1930s have become a commonplace among mainstream media commentators, and even more considered analysis by forums such as the Munich Security Conference, which declared in its recent, widely publicized 2018 report that the "liberal

---

[63] Between 2007 and 2012 the central governments of the G-7 nations took on additional liabilities equivalent to about two-fifths of their economic output, raising their gross debt-to-GDP ratio 50 percent (from 81.7 to 123.3 percent), and their net debt-to-GDP ratio an even more staggering 73 percent (from 49.7 to 85.3 percent). *Fiscal Reference Tables*, Department of Finance, Canada, September 2015, accessed February 20, 2018, https://www.fin.gc.ca/frt-trf/2015/frt-trf-15-eng.asp.

international order . . . institutions and norms conceived in the aftermath of World War II and largely shaped by the United States" is not only "under increasing pressure," but in "crisis."[64] Especially amid Russia's stress on the preservation of a sphere of influence (underlined by its military actions in the Caucasus, Ukraine, Syria); China's economic reorientation inward, and greater regional assertiveness (not least in territorial disputes like those regarding the Spratlys, the Senkakus and Bhutan); the troubles of the European Union (exemplified by British withdrawal); and sharpened American economic nationalism (just expressed in the announcement of new steel and aluminum tariffs); it seems plausible

---

[64] Michael Auslin, "China Takes Asia Back to the 1930s" *Wall Street Journal*, July 20, 2016, accessed February 20, 2018, https://www.wsj.com/articles/china-takes-asia-back-to-the-1930s-1469032195; George F. Will, "Vladimir Putin is Bringing Back the 1930s," *New York Times*, October 7, 2016, accessed February 20, 2018, https://www.washingtonpost.com/opinions/global-opinions/vladimir-putin-is-bringing-back-the-1930s/2016/10/07/0d91a1c8-8c0a-11e6-875e-2c1bfe943b66_story.html?utm_term=.729ce53f8b93; Jonathan Freedland, "The 1930s Were Humanity's Darkest, Bloodiest Hour. Are You Paying Attention?" *Guardian*, March 11, 2017, accessed February 20, 2018, https://www.theguardian.com/society/2017/mar/11/1930s-humanity-darkest-bloodiest-hour-paying-attention-second-world-war. The Conference's 2018 report begins by remarking "increasing concern about the stability of the so-called liberal international order . . . institutions and norms conceived in the aftermath of World War II and largely shaped by the United States," among them "international institutions and an open economic order, elements which have since served as the building blocks of international order." To the Brink and Back?" *Munich Security Report* 2018, Munich Security Conference, 6. Accessed February 21, at https://www.securityconference.de/en/discussion/munich-security-report/.

that a pattern of diminished engagement with the system, in favor of more exclusive, smaller-scale economic spaces, is underway.[65]

Given the dimmed prospects for economic growth in the coming years in the view of even the most orthodox institutions, and the prospect of new financial shocks, or worsening resource or environmental shocks, it is far from implausible that the situation could worsen, especially in the absence of ameliorative action.[66] One obvious prospect for such amelioration would, of course, be a line of economic development that offered greater returns, while ameliorating the dangers of the more plausible and threatening shocks. Clearly this is easier said than done, with many avenues of such growth less plausible than before. The repetition of anything comparable to the unique experience of the mid-century period—the opportunities they provided for economic stimulus, and the social changes they set in motion—is unforeseeable at the present time. The aforementioned trends in technological development, resource use and finance can also seem discouraging.

However, recent technological developments may offer some basis for both growth, and the amelioration of resource stress. The limitations previously discussed, from the unique one-time

---

[65] For a discussion of China's turn from the export-led strategy see Richard M. Cooper, "Can China's High Growth Continue?" in *The China Questions*, 119-125; Dwight H. Perkins, "Is the Chinese Economy Headed Toward a Hard Landing?" in *The China Questions*, 129-132; Jun Zhang, *The End of Hyper Growth in China?* (New York: Palgrave Macmillan, 2016).

[66] For an example of such projections, see Henrik Braconier, Giuseppe Nicoletti and Ben Westmore, *Policy Challenges for the Next Fifty Years*, Economic Policy Paper No. 9, Organization for Economic Cooperation and Development, July 2014. Accessed February 27, 2018, http://www.oecd-ilibrary.org/docserver/download/5jz18gs5fckf-en.pdf?expires=1519734889&id=id&accname=guest&checksum=1631C903DD42DF2052D6D97D83C48D3D.

boosts provided by many historically recent technologies, to the challenges facing the scientific community, ought not to be slighted, but are not necessarily irremediable. Certainly the manner in which scientific work has been organized and funded has been subject to wide criticism—particularly the impact of public sector austerity and business short-termism on research, and associated pressures that have contributed significantly to poor-quality research in areas like medicine.[67] Indeed, there may be areas of particular underinvestment resulting from perverse market incentives (like misuse of subsidies), excess pessimism, or both. Renewable energy is, for the time being, an area of increasing returns rather than diminishing ones, with sources such as photovoltaic solar and wind seeing their market price drop and their EROEI rise, to the point that they have become a cheaper means of generating electricity than even coal-fired plants, which is leading to a belated rush of investment dollars into the sector.

However, as yet the share of the world's energy generated by such sources has scarcely changed, fossil fuels continuing to account for five-sixths of world energy production. Additionally, increased consumption of oil, gas and even coal has not wholly been ruled out even as renewable energy output rises, given the opposition of vested interests, and thus far imperfect resolution of some of the problems involved in fully scaling up renewables (like large-scale storage of electricity). The result is that genuinely robust public backing of the sector would seem justified. A serious effort in this area will entail not merely R & D funding to refine existing methods of energy production (like photovoltaic solar and wind), and develop those in a much less advanced position today (like tidal, wind energy and algal biofuels), but also the associated infrastructure (flexible, efficient grids and storage capacity). Moreover, where the market does not readily supply it, it would also mean action to actually

---

[67] Richard Harris, *Rigor Mortis: How Sloppy Science Creates Worthless Cures, Crushes Hopes and Wastes Billions* (New York: Basic Books, 2017).

install, in rapid fashion, capacity based on these sources. All of this would be aided considerably by investment in up-to-date, energy efficient infrastructure and transport systems, helping bring demand in line with the growing supply at an earlier date. Meanwhile, given the high levels of greenhouse gases already in the atmosphere; the disruption they are already causing, and the likelihood of its worsening, even without additional emissions; and the increased accumulation of such gases likely to occur during even the most rapid practicable shift away from fossil fuels; it seems a near-certainty that a program not just to reduce emissions but to recapture past emissions will be essential to stabilizing the climate—a program especially likely to require public support on an international scale.

The computing sector may also be looking at genuinely transformative advances. Advances in the design of neural networks have facilitated "machine learning" sufficient to enable pattern recognition in regard to voice, image and other data, and the performance of tasks such as driving vehicles down city streets, with a competence rivaling or exceeding that of a human.[68] Even at what may be only an early phase in such development (and in spite of the weak macroeconomic conditions), manufacturers have rapidly expanded their use of factory robots, sales of which rose 12 percent a year in 2010-2016, with many estimates projecting their deployment accelerating in the next decade, and wide expectation of fully autonomous vehicles on the market within the same time

---

[68] Allison Linn, "Historic Achievement: Microsoft Researchers Reach Parity in Conversational Speech Recognition," *The A.I. Blog*, Microsoft, October 18, 2016, accessed February 20, 2018, https://blogs.microsoft.com/ai/historic-achievement-microsoft-researchers-reach-human-parity-conversational-speech-recognition/; Gideon Lewis-Kraus, "The Great A.I. Awakening," *New York Times*, December 14, 2016, accessed February 20, 2018, https://www.nytimes.com/2016/12/14/magazine/the-great-ai-awakening.html.

frame.[69] In short, artificial intelligence and robotics may well be in the process of bursting through the limitations Gordon identified, and accordingly laying the foundations for a productivity revolution in the foreseeable future.

It is conceivable, and indeed plausible, that these different endeavors can complement and reinforce one another—with one research team recently demonstrating one possibility by developing a method for transforming ambient carbon into ultra-light, ultra-strong carbon nanotubes, in a process powered by renewable energy, at far lower cost than the conventional methods of producing them.[70] Those nanotubes, in turn, have numerous industrial uses applicable to these specific areas—among them their conversion into "yarn" which can be used to generate electricity from renewable sources like wave action, and lower the weight of vehicle bodies, rendering them more energy-efficient, while becoming the preferred substrate for the next generation of faster, more powerful computers supporting the information processing load of increasingly advanced artificial intelligence.[71]

---

[69] Jonathan Vanian, "The Multi-Billion Dollar Robotics Market is About to Boom," *Forbes*, February 24, 2016, accessed February 20, 2018, http://fortune.com/2016/02/24/robotics-market-multi-billion-boom/.

[70] Lisa Zyga, "Cleaning Up CO2 Emissions Could Be Worth Millions," *Phys.org*, July 19, 2017, accessed February 20, 2018, https://phys.org/news/2017-07-co2-emissions-worth-millions.html.

[71] Stefanie Harvey, "Carbon Nanotube Technology Promises Revolution in Energy and Manufacturing," white paper, Transformative Connectivity, accessed February 20, 2018, http://www.te.com/content/dam/te-com/documents/aerospace-defense-and-marine/white-papers/harvey-carbon-nanotube-technology.pdf; Andrew Wagner, "These Tangled Carbon Nanotubes Can Harvest Energy Directly From Breathing and Ocean Waves," *Science* August 24, 2017, accessed February 20, 2018, https://www.sciencemag.org/news/2017/08/these-tangled-carbon-nanotubes-can-harvest-energy-directly-breathing-and-ocean-

Of course, even assuming that these technologies realize all that is hoped for them—like cheap, sustainable energy and a prolonged surge of productivity growth—they would be at best a partial solution to the problem, and would in their way raise their own problems. Most obviously, the productivity growth revival that artificial intelligence may bring on would seem likely to lead to massive displacement of labor, in the absence of new social and political arrangements contrary to the neoliberal trend that has prevailed in policymaking for four decades. However, at the very least they would provide a technological foundation for progress.

---

waves; Max Shulaker, Philip Wong and Subhasish Mitra, "How We'll Put a Carbon Nanotube Computer in Your Hand," *IEEE Spectrum*, June 30, 2016, accessed February 20, 2018, https://spectrum.ieee.org/semiconductors/devices/how-well-put-a-carbon-nanotube-computer-in-your-hand.

Revisiting the Evidence: A Supplementary Note on GDP Estimates

When recently updating the line of inquiry I first followed in my 2004 *International Security* article ("Societal Complexity and Diminishing Returns in Security") in "Rising Complexity, Diminishing Returns, Shrinking Slack: Revisiting the Evidence" (published via *SSRN* in March 2018), I made extensive use of the then-current data on Gross World Product.[1] However, all three of the sources on which I have relied for GWP data—the World Trade Organization (WTO), the Maddison Project and the United Nations (UN)—have since released new time series', the Maddison and UN updates their first in several years.[2] (In the case of the Maddison Project's uniquely lengthy series, the data is its first new set in five years.) Accordingly it seemed appropriate to examine those figures, and consider any bearing they might have on my argument. I also decided to examine the 1960-2015 World Bank (WB) data in this

---

[1] See Nader Elhefnawy, "Societal Complexity and Diminishing Returns in Security," *International Security* 29 No.1 (Summer 2004): 153-154; Nader Elhefnawy, "Rising Complexity, Diminishing Returns, Shrinking Slack," *SSRN*, 16 Mar. 2018.

[2] See World Trade Organization, "World Merchandise Exports and Gross Domestic Product," *World Trade Statistical Review 2017*, A55; Maddison Project Database, version 2018. Bolt, Jutta, Robert Inklaar, Herman de Jong and Jan Luiten van Zanden, "Rebasing 'Maddison': New Income Comparisons and the Shape of Long-run Economic Development," Maddison Project, Working Paper No. 10, 2018; United Nations, "Per Capita GDP at Constant 2010 Prices in U.S. Dollars," *National Accounts Main Aggregates Database*, Dec. 2017; United Nations, "Per Capita GDP in U.S. Dollars," *National Accounts Main Aggregates Database*, Dec. 2017.

survey.[3] Accordingly this supplementary note to "Rising Complexity" presents in systematic fashion the estimates of GWP growth I made from this data, and then discusses their implications.

As it happens, the WTO and Maddison-based estimates generally indicate a 3 percent a year growth rate during the post-war boom period, a reading more fragmentarily supported by the estimates derived from the WB and UN constant dollar figures (Table 1). All of them also show a slowdown during the 1970s, which worsened in the 1980s, and hit bottom in the first half of the 1990s (just a little over a half percent a year according to these four sets) (Table 2). However, the growth rate turned up in the late 1990s (Table 3). If less impressive than the best of the post-war boom, it was still a marked improvement over what was seen in most of the 1973-1995 period, and remained robust until 2008. After that point, amid a global financial crisis, the trend fell off again, but seems to have recovered after 2012. A decade by decade comparison of the data confirms this image (Table 4).

However, a different pattern is indicated by the estimates I derived from UN and World Bank current dollar data, which I adjusted for inflation and population growth (Tables 5 through 8).[4] These data, while admittedly more fragmentary in their pre-1973

---

[3] World Bank, "GDP Per Capita (Constant 2010 US$)," World Bank National Accounts Data and OECD National Accounts Data Files; World Bank, "GDP Per Capita (Currents US$)," World Bank National Accounts Data and OECD National Accounts Data Files.

[4] Alan Freeman took a similar approach to an IMF time series, with comparable results, in "Globalization: the End of an Era." In Ann Pettifor, ed., *Real World Economic Outlook* (Basingstoke: Palgrave MacMillan, 2003), 152-164. For my calculations I based the inflation rate on changes in year-end (December) dollar values as indicated by the U.S. Bureau of Labor Statistics' Consumer Price Index-based inflation calculator, and the population growth rate on the table provided by the U.S. Census Bureau's Mid-Year Population estimates for the world.

coverage, indicate even more impressive growth in this era than the conventional estimates. The UN figures indicate the post-1973 growth trend was still weaker, while the World Bank figures, if comparable to their constant dollar data overall, present a very different *pattern* of growth during the era from the estimates derived from the constant dollar figures provided by the very same organizations (presented in Tables 9 and 10, respectively).

Both the data sets based on UN and WB current dollar information present growth in the 1973-1980 period as stronger than the other estimates give it credit for being, offset by growth in the 1980s and 1990s being weaker. Indeed, the estimates based on UN data indicate that the 1980-2000 period saw the world's per capita GWP *shrink*, while the WB data indicates something only slightly better (a mere 0.4 percent a year growth rate for the whole two decades) (Table 5). This is partly because of their weaker estimates of GWP growth during the 1980s (a mere 0.2 percent a year in the UN-based figures), but also an even more divergent picture of the 1990s, presenting a surprisingly strong patch of growth in the first half of the decade, and a sharp economic contraction in the second (in the range of 2 percent a year).

Where the twenty-first century is concerned the estimates derived from the UN and WB current dollar figures present an even stronger than usual estimate of growth for the 2000-2008 period (well over 4 percent a year, more than double the constant dollar estimates of the same organization, and without parallel since the post-war boom years). However, they also present an even less happy picture of the aftermath. While presenting an estimate of anemic growth in the 2008-2012 identical to the constant dollar estimates (0.8 percent a year), they have the trend worsening rather than improving after 2012. Rather than a rebound in growth rates, what they present is the world economy contracting yet again, at rates comparable to those of the late '90s (2 percent a year or more).

Admittedly, the disagreement between the two sets is so large as to make them mutually exclusive—while the fact that the

Consumer Price Index is routinely attacked as overstating inflation by orthodox economists may make it seem that the error must be on the side of the inflation-adjusted current dollar estimates.[5] However, the disparity at least suggests a possibility that the more mainstream figures have understated the problem. It also raises questions about the bright spots analysts conventionally take for granted. At least in the United States the late 1990s are commonly thought of as boom times—the best of the post-1973 period. However, the UN and World Bank figures cited indicate such a dismal situation in the 1980-2000 in part because each identifies the late '90s as a period of severe global economic contraction.

As it happens, the particulars of the era would seem to easily explain that movement. Despite evidence of some real productivity gains in this period, that boom was substantially a matter of inflated asset prices.[6] Moreover, in the rest of the world the performance was often dismal—the late 1990s including as they did the latter part of Japan's "lost decade," the 1997-1998 Asian financial crisis, the low point of the post-Soviet sphere's economic collapse, and the continued debt crisis depressions of Latin America and Africa. Thus it does not seem terribly implausible to think the global growth record in this period was especially poor.

The same goes for how the post-2008 period, and especially the post-2012 period, is usually discussed. Explanations for the downturn in world performance, as opposed to the usual image of its turning upward after the crisis, are easy to find. Far and away the most obvious is that China, the single largest economy in Purchasing Power Parity terms, and the locomotive of the world economy in preceding years, at this point began its slowdown, without compensating performance anywhere else.

---

[5] Floyd Norris, "What Happens if Inflation is Overstated?" *New York Times* 9 Jun. 2006.

[6] See Robert J. Gordon, *The Rise and Fall of American Growth: The U.S. Standard of Living Since the Civil War* (Princeton, NJ: Princeton University Press, 2016), 17, 575.

By contrast the upturns to which the current dollar figure-based estimates point are more difficult to correlate with actual progress. The early 1990s, certainly, seem an unlikely boom period, given performance North and South, East and West, developed and developing, longtime capitalist and newly post-Communist. Moreover, the extraordinary growth these figures report for the 2000-2008 period seems readily explicable in terms of the exploding real estate, commodity and other asset prices that were a feature of the time. Accordingly, the constant dollar-based estimates seem the more plausible.

Responding to this fact by taking the growth estimates based on the UN current dollar series', and modifying what they show for the 1990-1995 and 2000-2008 periods in line with the growth rates suggested by the constant dollar estimates for the same period results in an annualized rate of 0.15 percent a year since 1980—a rough *tenth* of the growth rate suggested by the more conventional figures (Table 1), and scarcely above pre-industrial rates.[7] Such a method of treating the figures may seem questionable, and the result an overly pessimistic estimate of the post-1973 growth trend. However, even without taking this tack the data considered here does provide some reason to think its performance over the last four decades has been even worse than generally acknowledged, relative to the post-war boom years but also in absolute terms. It also offers grounds for regarding the post-2012 performance of the world economy as poorer than the rhetoric which generally paints the crisis of 2007-2008 as past.

All this also suggests that the host of factors that numerous analysts of the scene have identified as slowing the pace of growth (the disruptions of financial activity, ecological damage, etc.) have been even more damaging than has generally appreciated. Where my paper's argument is concerned—the tendency of modern

---

[7] Between 1000 and 1700 CE, the rate was 0.04 percent a year. See Angus Maddison, Maddison Project Database, version 2010.

civilization to investments in complexity to diminishing returns—it is that much more suggestive of the trend, and its implications, not least shrinking slack and a rising vulnerability to shocks, of which there have been no shortage in recent years, and which themselves often reflect such stresses. The resurgence of economic nationalism and right-wing populism (all evident in the U.S. election of 2016); increasing hostility to the European Union across the European space, the strongest example of which has been Britain's exit from the institution (2016); the flaring of secession crises below the nation-state level, most notably the attempt of Catalonia to secede from Spain (2017); intensified great power conflict between the West and Russia in Europe and the Middle East, and between the U.S., Japan and India on one side and China on the other in southern and eastern Asia and the western Pacific; and even the weakening of alliance systems, with the widening rift between the U.S. and Europe a case in point; all appear to be such.[8] Commonly treated as separate matters by commentators, they are all easily readable as expressions of worsening economic stress, to which they in turn seem likely to contribute.

---

[8] Regarding the last, see Roger Cohen, "The Moral Rot That Threatens America," *New York Times*, 18 May 2018.

TABLES

Table 1. Per Capita GWP Growth Rates, 1950-2015 (Annualized %)

Period	WTO	WB (Constant)	UN (Constant)	Maddison
1950-1973	3.2	N/A	N/A	3
1960-1973	3.5	3.5	N/A	3.2
1973-2015	1.4	1.4	1.4	1.6
1973-2008	1.5	1.5	1.5	1.7
1980-2000	1.4	1.3	1.3	1.2
2000-2015	1.4	1.5	1.5	2.3

Table 2. Per Capita GWP Growth Rates, 1970-1995 (Annualized %)

Period	WTO	WB (Constant)	UN (Constant)	Maddison
1970-1973	2.7	3.4	3.4	3.1
1973-1995	1.3	1.2	1.2	1.1
1973-1980	1.6	1.3	1.4	1.6
1980-1995	1.1	1.1	1.1	0.9
1990-1995	0.5	0.6	0.6	0.6

Table 3. Per Capita GWP Growth Rates, 1995-2015 (Annualized %)

Period	WTO	WB (Constant)	UN (Constant)	Maddison
1995-2015	1.6	1.7	1.7	2.2
1995-2008	1.9	2	2	2.5
1995-2000	2.2	2.1	2.1	2.2
2000-2015	1.4	1.5	1.5	2.3
2000-2008	1.2	1.9	1.9	2.8
2008-2015	1	1.1	1.1	1.8
2008-2012	0.4	0.8	0.8	1.7
2012-2015	1.7	1.6	1.6	2.1

Table 4. Per Capita GWP Growth Rates, By Decade, 1950-2015 (Annualized %)

Decade	WTO	WB (Constant)	UN (Constant)	Maddison
1950-1960	2.9	N/A	N/A	2.9
1960-1970	3.6	3.4	N/A	3.2
1970-1980	1.9	2	2	2.1
1980-1990	1.5	1.3	1.3	1
1990-2000	1.4	1.3	1.3	1.4
2000-2010	1.6	1.5	1.5	2.4
2010-2015	1.4	1.6	1.6	2

Table 5. Per Capita GWP Growth Rates, Current Dollar Estimates, 1960-2015 (Annualized %)

Period	UN (Current)	WB (Current)
1960-1973	N/A	3.9
1973-2015	1	1.4
1973-2008	1.3	1.5
1980-2000	-0.1<	0.4
2000-2015	2.1	2.2

Table 6. Per Capita GWP Growth Rates, Current Dollar Estimates, 1970-1995 (Annualized %)

Period	UN (Current)	WB (Current)
1970-1973	7.6	7.8
1973-1995	1	1.6
1973-1980	1.6	2.2
1980-1995	0.7	1.3
1990-1995	1.8	2

Table 7. Per Capita GWP Growth Rates, Current Dollar Estimates, 1995-2015 (Annualized %)

Period	UN (Current)	WB (Current)
1995-2015	0.2	1.1
1995-2008	0.6	1.9
1995-2000	-2.2	-2
2000-2015	2.1	2.2
2000-2008	4.6	4.5
2008-2015	-0.5	-0.5
2008-2012	0.8	0.8
2012-2015	-2.3	-2.1

Table 8. Per Capita GWP Growth Rates, Current Dollar Estimates,
By Decade, 1950-2015 (Annualized %)

Decade	UN (Current)	WB (Current)
1960-1970	N/A	2.9
1970-1980	3.4	3.8
1980-1990	0.2	0.9
1990-2000	-0.3	<0.1
2000-2010	3.3	3.3
2010-2015	-0.8	-0.1

Table 9. UN Per Capita GWP Growth Rates, Constant and Current
Dollar, 1970-2015 (Annualized %)

Period	Constant	Current
1970-1973	3.4	7.6
1973-2015	1.4	1
1973-2008	1.5	1.3
1973-1980	1.4	1.6
1980-2000	1.3	-0.1<
1980-1990	1.1	0.2
1990-2000	1.3	-0.3
1990-1995	0.6	1.8
1995-2000	2.1	-2.2
2000-2015	1.5	2.1
2000-2008	1.9	4.6
2008-2015	1.1	-0.5
2008-2012	0.8	0.8
2012-2015	1.2	-2.3

Table 10. WB Per Capita GWP Growth Rates, Constant and
Current Dollar, 1960-2015 (Annualized %)

Period	Constant	Current
1960-1973	3.5	3.9
1960-1970	3.4	2.9
1970-1973	3.4	7.8
1973-2015	1.4	1.4
1973-2008	1.5	1.5
1973-1980	1.3	2.2
1980-2000	1.3	0.4
1980-1990	1.3	0.9
1990-2000	1.3	<0.1
1990-1995	0.6	2
1995-2000	2.1	-2
2000-2015	1.5	2.2
2000-2008	1.9	4.5
2008-2015	1.1	-0.5
2008-2012	0.8	0.8
2012-2015	1.6	-2.1

An International System Under Stress?
A Complexity Theory-Based View

In the wake of the "Great Recession," the European Union's sovereign debt crisis, and the increasing frequency and severity of confrontation between Russia and China with neighboring states and the West, comparisons of present-day troubles with those of the 1930s have become a commonplace of mainstream media commentators, and even more considered analysis by forums such as the Munich Security Conference.[1] However, despite the

---

[1] Michael Auslin, "China Takes Asia Back to the 1930s" *Wall Street Journal*, July 20, 2016, accessed February 20, 2018, https://www.wsj.com/articles/china-takes-asia-back-to-the-1930s-1469032195; George F. Will, "Vladimir Putin is Bringing Back the 1930s," *New York Times*, October 7, 2016, accessed February 20, 2018, https://www.washingtonpost.com/opinions/global-opinions/vladimir-putin-is-bringing-back-the-1930s/2016/10/07/0d91a1c8-8c0a-11e6-875e-2c1bfe943b66_story.html?utm_term=.729ce53f8b93; Jonathan Freedland, "The 1930s Were Humanity's Darkest, Bloodiest Hour. Are You Paying Attention?" *Guardian*, March 11, 2017, accessed February 20, 2018, https://www.theguardian.com/society/2017/mar/11/1930s-humanity-darkest-bloodiest-hour-paying-attention-second-world-war. The Conference's 2018 report begins by remarking "increasing concern about the stability of the so-called liberal international order . . . institutions and norms conceived in the aftermath of World War II and largely shaped by the United States," among them "international institutions and an open economic order, elements which have since served as the building blocks of international order." To the Brink and Back?" *Munich Security Report* 2018,

widespread sense of the international scene as less stable and more troubled than before, mainstream writers have made few attempts to move beyond describing this trend to actually analyzing it. This article endeavors to offer such an analysis by way of Joseph Tainter's theory regarding "diminishing marginal returns on investments in societal complexity."[2] To that end it will examine the larger events and trends that have caused such concern, offer an overview of Tainter's theory, demonstrate its applicability to those events and trends, and consider their implications for present-day problems.

A Decade of Crises: A Comprehensive View
One attempt to chart the major trends of the post-Cold War world cited as three of the most notable trends of the 1990-2010 period the decline of great power conflict; the increased tendency of war to be fought below the interstate level, less intense, and confined to the margins of the global system; and the broadened and deepened integration of the global economy.[3] All three of these apparently epoch-defining trends now appear to be in retreat.

Great power conflict, confrontation, crisis have all become more frequent and intense than at any time since the mid-1980s. The last decade saw Russia's war with Georgia (2008) prove not a last gasp of old rivalries, but a foreshadowing of increasing conflict

---

Munich Security Conference, 6. Accessed February 21, at https://www.securityconference.de/en/discussion/munich-security-report/.

[2] Joseph Tainter, *The Collapse of Complex Societies* (New York: Cambridge University Press, 1988). Of course, complexity as such is not an end in itself. It can, in fact, be regarded as an unwanted byproduct of their strategies. Still, the term is useful because as a practical matter it is an outcome of responses like new regulations or specialized institutions for dealing with a problem.

[3] Nader Elhefnawy, "Twenty Years After the Cold War: A Strategic Survey," *Parameters* 41 No. 1 (Spring 2011): 6-17.

between Russia and the West in the invasion and annexation of the Crimea (2014), the proxy conflict in the Donbass (2014-), and the still more violent confrontation over Syria (2015-), which has seen clashes between ground forces involving hundreds of battle deaths between U.S. troops and Russian private military contractors (February 2018). Meanwhile China's conflicts with its neighbors over territorial claims in the South (2011-) and East China Seas (2012-) have resurged, while that country has had its sharpest confrontation with India in three decades over Bhutan (2017), in a pattern of less restrained and more assertive behavior that has undermined or even reversed decades of improving relations.[4]

These same years have also seen the U.S. and its allies devote greater attention to the possibility of military conflict with Russia and China, a shift strongly evident in recent changes to the U.S. *National Security Strategy*. Where the 2015 edition placed greater stress on such conflict than its 2010 predecessor, the 2017 document flatly declared that

> after being dismissed as a phenomenon of an earlier century, great power competition returned. China and Russia . . . reassert their influence regionally and globally . . . contesting our geopolitical advantages and trying to change the international order in their favor.[5]

---

[4] Odd Arne Westad, "Will China Lead Asia?" In *The China Questions*, ed. Jennifer Rudolph and Michael Szonyi (Cambridge, MA: Harvard University Press, 2018), 68-69.

[5] President of the United States, *National Security Strategy of the United States of America* (2017), 27. Accessed February 20, 2018, https://www.whitehouse.gov/wp-content/uploads/2017/12/NSS-Final-12-18-2017-0905.pdf. By contrast the 2010 edition stressed that "Europe is now more united, free, and at peace than ever before," and generally discussed relations with Russia and China in terms of its statement of intent "to deepen our cooperation with other 21st century centers of influence—including China . . .   and

Particularly where China is concerned, this tendency has been given substance in the "pivot" to East Asia (2012) in which the U.S. has concentrated its air and sea forces in the Asia-Pacific region.

At the same time, while neoliberal globalization has never been unchallenged, in the post-Cold War era overt, explicitly ideological challenges were generally confined to the system's margins (the opposition of populist Latin American governments), or within the core countries, the margins of their political systems (as has generally been the case with the anti-globalization movement).[6] However, in the wake of the extraordinary destruction

---

Russia—on the basis of mutual interests and mutual respect." The sole references to conflict with Russia and China are declarations that "[w]hile actively seeking Russia's cooperation to act as a responsible partner in Europe and Asia, we will support the sovereignty and territorial integrity of Russia's neighbors," and an American intention to "monitor China's military modernization program and prepare accordingly to ensure that U.S. interests and allies, regionally and globally, are not negatively affected." The word "aggression," not explicitly linked with any one state, is used only twice in the text. President of the United States, *National Security Strategy* (2010), 8, 11, 44, 43. Accessed February 20, 2018, http://nssarchive.us/NSSR/2010.pdf. By contrast the 2015 edition made no such sanguine statements about peace in Europe, while stressing the deterrence or imposition of costs on "Russian aggression" (a phrase used in the text no fewer than eight times, while implicitly referenced in other, more frequent use of the term "aggression"). President of the United States, *National Security Strategy* (2015), 2, 4, 19, 25. Accessed February 20, 2018, http://nssarchive.us/wp-content/uploads/2015/02/2015.pdf.

[6] By contrast, such affairs as the temporary imposition of higher steel tariffs by the United States in 2002, rescinded ahead of schedule in the wake of a World Trade Organization ruling against them and retaliatory threats from the European Union, were limited, non-ideological affairs—at most "cheating" rather than trying to challenge the arrangement.

of asset values during the 2008 financial crisis, and the subsequent anemic economic performance, skepticism in the West has led to a succession of political crises and even possible watershed events, like the exit of Britain from the European Union, and the 2016 election of Donald Trump President in the United States, both rejections of the "open economic order" and its associated institutions by major states unseen in generations. Indeed, in the wake of all these developments it has become common to claim, as the Munich Security Conference did in its widely publicized 2018 report does, that the "liberal international order . . . institutions and norms conceived in the aftermath of World War II and largely shaped by the United States" is not only "under increasing pressure," but in "crisis."[7]

The Theoretical Framework

Joseph Tainter's argument has run that the common pattern in the decay of "complex societies," whether of ancient or modern times, is investment in complexity to diminishing marginal returns. Put more concretely, societies solve problems old and new through adaptation in the form of "more institutions, more subgroups . . . more social roles, greater specialization, and more networks . . . more vertical and horizontal controls and a greater interdependence," organizing themselves more intricately to more effectively meet the challenges they set themselves.[8]

Of course, complexity is often a successful problem-solving approach. However, as implied in the very examples given above, complexity carries with it both costs and risks. More complexity, for

---

[7] "To the Brink and Back?" *Munich Security Report* 2018, Munich Security Conference, 6. Accessed February 21, 2018, at https://www.securityconference.de/en/discussion/munich-security-report/.

[8] Timothy F.H. Allen, Joseph A. Tainter and Thomas W. Hoekstra, *Supply-Side Sustainability* (New York: Columbia University Press, 2003), 62.

example, tends to carry a higher cost in terms of the energy and the information-processing required to sustain it. (An industrial society, for example, requires a large-scale exploitation of inanimate power sources and widespread literacy in order to function, whereas a less complex agrarian society does not.) The adaptation is conducted with information and decision-making processes that are in various ways imperfect, and may well have unforeseen and even unforeseeable, negative consequences. (That the pollution generated by industrialized societies might alter the Earth's climate was not a consideration in the nineteenth century.) Finally, societies can be overwhelmed, with the cost of having coped successfully with the last challenge possibly that of not having the resources to face the next crisis.[9] (Having exhausted its financial resources winning a war, a society might deprive itself of the means to secure the peace afterward, as arguably occurred in and after World War I.[10])

The mounting energy and information-processing cost can eventually come to exceed a society's means (for example, if it exhausts its energy supplies), while the burdens they were required to bear as the cost of past successes, anticipated (like financial burdens) or unanticipated (as with much pollution), can all make a particular pattern of adaptation "maladaptive" enough to eat into the return on investment, diminishing it or even rendering it negative. Such a trend necessarily depletes a society's slack—the "human and material buffering capacity" that enables it to expand, or endure

---

[9] For instance, internal-combustion vehicles solved a transportation problem, but had maladaptive effects in the form of pollution and a dependence on scarce fossil fuel resources. Murray Gell-Mann, "Complex Adaptive Systems," in *Complexity*, G. Cowan, D. Pines, and D. Meltzer, eds., (Cambridge, Massachusetts: Perseus Books, 1994), p. 22.

[10] See Nader Elhefnawy, "Rising Complexity, Diminishing Returns, Shrinking Slack: Revisiting the Evidence," working paper, SSRN, Mar. 16, 2018, 9-13. Accessed July 18, 2018, at https://ssrn.com/abstract=3142156.

shocks. Put in other terms, a society becomes stagnant and brittle. In the process it is likely to see increasing conflict among its members over its direction, and perhaps increasing dissatisfaction with it as insufficiently rewarding or worse leading to their rejecting it (through the evasion of obligations and rules, and even secession and rebellion). All of this eventually leaves it susceptible to collapse due to calamities that in an earlier, more dynamic period it would have been able to weather.

Thus did a once expanding Rome become increasingly unstable, conflict-ridden and ultimately vulnerable to the "barbarian" invasions of the fourth and fifty centuries CE. And thus, Tainter argues, might societies go today, modern, industrial societies apparently traveling along a similar path of diminishing, slack-eroding marginal returns on their investments in complexity.[11] Putting this into more comprehensive terms, one can argue that not merely individual, industrialized states face this trend, but the international economic system as a whole.[12]

Of course, it is one thing to assert that all this is happening, another to demonstrate it. One has to demonstrate that the world is becoming more complex; and that it is doing so to such diminishing returns and such eroding slack. However, complexity is, by and large, a matter of information content, specifically the amount of information necessary to model or operate a given system.[13] A case

---

[11] Joseph Tainter, *The Collapse of Complex Societies* (New York: Cambridge University Press, 1988) 91-126, 209-216. According to his definition, complexity refers to "asymmetric relationships that reflect organization and restraint" between the parts of a system. Important characteristics of complex systems include large numbers of densely interconnected, highly interdependent components and nonlinear functioning.

[12] Elhefnawy, "Rising."

[13] Philosopher Nicholas Rescher suggests four broad categories: formulaic complexity; compositional complexity; structural complexity; and functional complexity. These refer, respectively, to

can also be made that economic growth can be treated as a measure of returns on those investments in complexity; and that the financial and fiscal strain suggested by rising debt levels, and especially in the public sector, evident in the combination of rising debt levels with an inability to increase taxes or reduce spending, indicate shrinking slack (at least, in the fiscal-macroeconomic area).[14]

A very great deal of data indicates that this has all been very much the case. Given the world's expanding population and material output; the growing volume and evolving structure of trade and investment; the rising flows of long-distance travel and communication, and growing volume of information recording and processing; and the enlarged share of capital, income and labor

---

the volume of information needed to describe or produce a system, or resolve a given problem; the number or variety of elements within a system; the number, variety and elaborateness of relationships between those elements; and the number, variety and intricacy of a system's functioning. Nicholas Rescher, *Complexity: A Philosophical Overview* (New Brunswick, N.J.: Transaction Publishers, 1998), p. 9. These various types of complexity, however, while theoretically separable, tend to run together in practice; in every respect, a space shuttle is a far more complex machine than the Wright Brothers' Flyer.

[14] One can argue for at least four different *kinds* of societal slack. The first is fiscal-macroeconomic, namely the economic (and especially, financial and monetary) resources societies can call on in time of need to achieve a given end; the industrial-technological slack inhering in existing infrastructure and other physical assets to do the same; human resources slack, in the form of the labor and skills that can be deployed for such purposes; and political-cultural slack, the collective willingness of societies to act in the ways described above. Nader Elhefnawy, "A Long-Term Trend Toward the Depletion of Fiscal-Macroeconomic Slack?" working paper, SSRN, 31 May 2018, 2-3. Accessed July 18, 2018, at https://papers.ssrn.com/sol3/papers.cfm?abstract_id=3182381.

devoted to these activities; it seems impossible to deny that the world's complexity is rising sharply.

Meanwhile, it is notable that where in its first decades the present, post-World War II system underwent a boom of intensity and duration unprecedented in human history, the decades from the 1970s on have seen a marked slowing of growth, down to a fraction of its earlier, post-war boom rate.[15] These decades have also seen increasing financial and fiscal strain in the form of massively enlarged private and public debt, reflecting both that weakened growth trend, and the inability of states, and private actors, to constrain that growth.[16] This period has also seen an increased tendency toward financial crisis, with the decade since the 2007-2008 financial crisis seeing a great leap in the expansion of public debt in particular, and the further depression of the long-term growth outlook.[17]

Rising Political Stress?

As noted earlier, when the actors in a system find it insufficiently rewarding, it sees less participation and more conflict. Given the fact of weakening growth and rising fiscal strain—of diminishing marginal returns and shrinking slack for decades—one would expect to see evidence of both, perhaps especially after the economic turmoil of the last decade. And indeed there has been an increase in both disengagement and conflict, which can be connected with states' experience of economic frustrations and an increased emphasis on smaller, presumably more manageable economic spaces. Russia and China are each obvious examples. Both countries became capitalist, and went so far as to join the World Trade Organization (China in 2001, Russia in 2011), but

---

[15] Elhefnawy, "A Long-Term Trend," 4-7; "Rising Complexity," 13-14.

[16] Elhefnawy, "A Long-Term Trend," 7-11; "Rising Complexity," 14-16.

[17] Elhefnawy, "Rising Complexity," 13-16.

both, if not dramatically breaking with the system, have in significant ways reacted defensively against it, and sought to create conditions in which such a turn could be carried through more fully.

Russia arguably began such a shift following the financial shock of 1997-1998 that at the time was touted as an object lesson of the perils of integration into the world economy, and pushed the country into default. Since that time its economic strategy rested on exploiting strategic resources that, due to their inseparability from territorial control, highly uneven global distribution and inelasticity of demand, lend themselves exceptionally well to instrumentalization as tools of state power—oil and gas. Moreover, while less publicized than the use of its largely oil and gas-derived revenues to rehabilitate its armed forces, Russia pointedly pursued an expansion of its slack—by paying off international debt, and amassing one of the world's most formidable reserves of hard currency (some $600 billion in 2008). That reserve served the Russian government as a buffer through the post-2008 drop in the price of oil, and the larger economic crisis, since which time Russia has used its continuing revenues to rebuild that same reserve (amassing in it $400 billion by 2017). Additionally, Russia's highly publicized military actions (in the Caucasus, Ukraine and Syria) have been strongly connected with its interests as an oil exporter, and the preservation or reinforcement of a larger economic and political sphere more generally.[18] Also an expression of an increased prioritization of a space relatively protected against the intrusions of the bigger system has been Russia's role as a founding member, with several other former Soviet republics in Central Asia (Kazakhstan, Kyrgyzstan, Tajikistan and Uzbekistan), and the People's Republic of China, of a Eurasian community in the Shanghai Cooperation Organization (SCO) in 2001.

---

[18] While not itself a scene of significant energy supplies, Ukraine was of significance as a pipeline route, while Russia's naval position in the country was crucial to its ability to operate militarily in the Mediterranean—as it did when intervening in Syria.

In contrast with Russia, China began its economic reform process a decade earlier (and acceded to the WTO a decade earlier), has been a commodity importer rather than exporter, formally oriented itself toward global manufacturing exports, and enjoyed longer, more rapid and more sustained growth, which at present remains relatively rapid. All that may suggest its being less likely to follow such a strategy. Still, China's amassing of vast foreign reserves through mercantilist policies, and its cofounding of the SCO, reflect its following comparable imperatives in the economic sphere to a considerable degree. It is also notable that recent years have seen the exhaustion of China's longtime export-led growth strategy by its increasing development, and the diminished prospects for global growth generally post-2008, forcing a reconsideration of its approach. This was promptly followed by increased attention to internal rather than foreign demand, while the country took a harder line on territorial disputes with its neighbors.[19]

Indicative of an even deeper shift away from global engagement toward smaller, more manageable economic spaces has been the fraying of even their regionally integrative institutions implied in the maneuvering within their jointly created bloc.

---

[19] Simply because of the weight it has already achieved, future export growth can no longer give the country's economy a major boost; while hopes that increased internal consumption can easily provide alternative demand for its output may be overstated. Certainly its Keynesian stimulus, which entailed massive investment in transport and construction, and indirectly, the associated "supplier" industries, had results that were mixed at best, holding recession at bay but at the price of excess capacity, falling productivity and falling profits. See Richard M. Cooper, "Can China's High Growth Continue?" in *The China Questions*, 119-125; Dwight H. Perkins, "Is the Chinese Economy Headed Toward a Hard Landing?" in *The China Questions*, 129-132; Jun Zhang, *The End of Hyper Growth in China?* (New York: Palgrave Macmillan, 2016).

Russia's support for India's entry into the SCO has widely been read as an attempt to counterbalance the far greater economic weight China has acquired since the institution's founding, while China has supported Pakistan's entry as an offset to India.[20] The preoccupation with counterbalancing within the organization, and the prospect of its dilution as a vehicle for promoting the interests of its principals, implies a sense of frustration in the results of even regional-level engagement, and indeed, a retreat into still narrower nationalism.

The tendency has also been quite evident in the West itself, with the most striking example the departure of the United Kingdom from the European Union, an event unprecedented in the history of the organization. While refracted through the flux of their party systems, other EU states have seen long-marginalized or only newly founded parties (France's National Front; Germany's Alternative for Germany; Italy's Five-Star Movement and Forza Italia) achieve gains or even capture power at the expense of the major, establishment parties on the basis of an anti-EU platform.

While today less advanced and unambiguous, the same trend has been evident in what is not only the largest world economy in nominal terms, but the principal creator and promoter of the post-

---

[20] Alexander Cooley, "In Central Asia, Public Cooperation and Private Rivalry," *New York Times*, June 8, 2012, accessed February 20, 2018, http://www.nytimes.com/2012/06/09/opinion/in-central-asia-public-cooperation-and-private-rivalry.html; Derek Grossman, "China Will Regret India's Entry into the Shanghai Cooperation Organization," *The Diplomat*, July 24, 2017, accessed February 20, 2018, https://thediplomat.com/2017/07/china-will-regret-indias-entry-into-the-shanghai-cooperation-organization/; Salvator Babones, "Why is Democratic India Joining Russia and China's 'Anti-Western' Club, the SCO," *Forbes* 29 Nov. 2017, accessed February 20, 2018, https://www.forbes.com/sites/salvatorebabones/2017/11/29/why-is-democratic-india-joining-russia-and-chinas-anti-western-club-the-sco/#44dcbcb24cac.

World War II order, the United States. The 2016 U.S. presidential election saw an upsurge of economic nationalist rhetoric among major candidates of both the principal parties—Democrat Senator Bernard Sanders, as well as the Republican Donald Trump. Following his election (which has been attributed by many to the Democrats sidelining Sanders in favor of the more orthodox Hillary Clinton), Trump withdrew the U.S. from the nascent Trans-Pacific Partnership. He also unsettled existing arrangements, initiating an attempt to renegotiate the North American Free Trade Agreement, and openly discussing a significant elevation of tariffs directed not just against particular products (like steel), but major U.S. trading partners (like China and Mexico). This has been underlined by his explicit declaration of intent to ignore the inevitable disapproval of the WTO if and when such policies actually materialize.[21]

In contrast with the events of the interwar period these trends have advanced to only a limited degree, but the point is that with events like "Brexit" and the recent announcements in U.S. trade policy, the shift is going beyond mere rhetoric, and it does not seem at all implausible to consider the prospect of its continuation, especially if the stresses described above also continue (or worsen), as is widely expected.

All of this suggests that this will be the trend of future developments, with implications for efforts to expand or more thoroughly integrate the European Union (and perhaps the Shanghai Cooperation Organization as well). More serious, it suggests an increased accent on spheres of influence that, while likely to be quite mild compared to the turn of the interwar period for some time to come, while already producing a disturbingly increased frequency

---

[21] Damian Paletta and Ana Swanson, "Trump Suggests Ignoring World Trade Organization in Major Policy Shift," *Washington Post*, March 1, 2017, accessed February 20, 2018, https://www.washingtonpost.com/news/wonk/wp/2017/03/01/trump-may-ignore-wto-in-major-shift-of-u-s-trade-policy/?utm_term=.09d022587d04.

and severity of international confrontations and crises. Moreover, the economic and political stress alike can easily be exacerbated by highly plausible, even probable new shocks, like a new round of financial crisis, or an especially sharp resource or environmental shock.

A fragmenting, more crisis-ridden international system cannot be regarded with equanimity. Moreover, while no one can dispute that more careful management of a sharply altered and more difficult set of international relationships is essential, such management falls far short of a complete redress of the situation. The larger, longer-term danger and its roots make the pursuit of two necessary and interlinked objects imperative—reviving growth, while at the same time ameliorating the dangers of the more plausible and threatening shocks. Clearly this is easier said than done, with many avenues of such growth (like the cheap resource-driven "extensive" growth of the past) less plausible than before, and at the same time, the potential severity of the shocks increasingly forbidding, but that makes the matter no less pressing.

A Long-Term Trend Toward The Depletion of Fiscal-Macroeconomic Slack in the World Economy?

Slack can be defined as that "human and material buffering capacity" enabling social and technological systems "to absorb unpredicted, and often unpredictable, shocks."[1] Besides providing a cushion, it is also what enables systems, be they an ecology, a corporation or a country, to seize new opportunities, fulfill new roles, and grow.

Archaeologist Joseph Tainter has argued that industrial societies are in the process of depleting their slack through diminishing marginal returns on investment in complexity.[2] Such a position may seem counterintuitive, since complexity is a way of adapting systems in problem-solving ways, and one which typically succeeds. Nonetheless, adaptation is conducted with imperfect information and decision-making processes, and adaptive capabilities are not infinite; they can be overwhelmed, and the cost

---

[1] Gene I. Rochlin, *Trapped in the Net: The Unanticipated Consequences of Computerization* (Princeton, New Jersey: Princeton University Press, 1999), p. 213.

[2] Joseph Tainter, *The Collapse of Complex Societies* (New York: Cambridge University Press, 1988) 91-126, 209-216. According to his definition, complexity refers to "asymmetric relationships that reflect organization and restraint" between the parts of a system. Important characteristics of complex systems include large numbers of densely interconnected, highly interdependent components and nonlinear functioning.

of having coped successfully with the last challenge may be not having the resources to face the next crisis.[3] More generally, solutions to one problem often have "maladaptive" effects that exacerbate others.

Compelling and widely applicable as Tainter's theory is, it nonetheless remains to be proven that there is increasing investment in complexity; and that it is having these effects. In attempting this it has to be acknowledged that measuring complexity is a difficult and controversial matter, reflected in the fact that there are literally dozens of such yardsticks, specialized for fields of human activity ranging from linguistics to physics.[4] However, their common denominator is information content, specifically the amount of information necessary to model or operate a given system.[5]

---

[3] For instance, internal-combustion vehicles solved a transportation problem, but had maladaptive effects in the form of pollution and a dependence on scarce fossil fuel resources. Murray Gell-Mann, "Complex Adaptive Systems," in *Complexity*, G. Cowan, D. Pines, and D. Meltzer, eds., (Cambridge, Massachusetts: Perseus Books, 1994), p. 22.

[4] Seth L. Loyal, quoted in John Horgan, *The End of Science* (Reading, MA: Addison-Wesley, 1996), p. 288.

[5] Philosopher Nicholas Rescher suggests four broad categories: formulaic complexity; compositional complexity; structural complexity; and functional complexity. These refer, respectively, to the volume of information needed to describe or produce a system, or resolve a given problem; the number or variety of elements within a system; the number, variety and elaborateness of relationships between those elements; and the number, variety and intricacy of a system's functioning. Nicholas Rescher, *Complexity: A Philosophical Overview* (New Brunswick, N.J.: Transaction Publishers, 1998), p. 9. These various types of complexity, however, while theoretically separable, tend to run together in practice; in every respect, a space shuttle is a far more complex machine than the Wright Brothers' Flyer.

If one goes by information content, there can be little doubt that the complexity of human civilization is steadily increasing. The world's expanding population and material output; the growing volume and increasingly intricate structure of trade and investment; the rising flows of long-distance travel and communication; the enlarged share of capital, income and labor devoted to information processing; provides ample statistical support to the intuitive conclusion that complexity is increasing, and markedly.[6]

It is a less simple matter to demonstrate that investment in these areas is actually producing the diminishing marginal returns Tainter wrote about; and that this is leading to the depletion of slack-particularly at the global level. However, one can argue that the performance of the advanced economies, and the world economy as a whole, can demonstrate the former, with a falling rate of economic growth classifying as a fall in such returns.

Measuring the depletion (or accumulation) of societal slack is more difficult, since even at the level of individual countries or the global economy as a whole, it seems possible to speak of at least four different *kinds* of societal slack. The first is fiscal-macroeconomic, namely the economic (and especially, financial and monetary) resources societies can call on to achieve a given end in time of need. The second is industrial-technological, or the flexibility inhering in existing infrastructure and other physical assets to do the same.[7] The third, human resources slack, is the reserve of labor and skills that can be deployed for such purposes. The fourth is political-cultural, or in other words, the collective willingness of societies to act in the ways described above.

---

[6] Nader Elhefnawy, "Societal Complexity and Diminishing Returns in Security," *International Security* 29.1 (Summer 2004), pp. 155-156.

[7] It may be reasonable to speak in terms of ecological-natural resource lack, but where economic production is concerned, this is very hard to disentangle from the technological base exploiting those resources.

One can only go so far in distinguishing between them, some overlap being inevitable, but this article will concentrate on discussing the first kind of slack, which seems to be the most susceptible to measurement. In exploring this, it will concentrate on the pattern of savings and debt, these being good indicators of the slack existing in an economy. Falling savings, mounting debt and tighter finances (relative to the size of the economy) all indicate fewer unused resources (perhaps absolutely, but certainly relatively, and it is the relative rise or fall of this kind of slack with which this article is concerned) which can be called on in time of need, and can therefore be interpreted as a reduction of slack, with specifically public finances held to be especially revealing, and warranting particularly close examination here.

The global data apart, the focus will be on the major advanced states because they arguably represent the furthest development of complexity in the modern world, and its implications; because they account for the larger part of the world's total economic output, and thus a disproportionate share of the functioning of the system overall; and because they have been the most thoroughly studied to date, so that more data is available, and the analyst of that data can be more confident of their examination of it. After its survey of the data relevant to these areas, the article will then move on to assessing the data for its implications, and possible explanations for this case of affairs.

Falling Economic Growth

Measured in constant 2000 dollars, the Gross Domestic Product (GDP) of the United States grew at an annualized rate of 4.2 percent a year from 1950-1973, then 2 percent a year from 1974-1995 according to Bureau of Economic Analysis data (Table 1). According to the same time series, growth picked up again after that, rising to 3.2 percent a year in the 1995-2000 period, but falling back down to rate of 2.3 percent a year for 2000-2008 after adjustment for inflation.

Adjusting the data for population growth actually makes the drop more pronounced. The rate of per-capita growth for the 1950-1973 period was 2.6-2.7 percent a year, fell to 1 percent in the years 1973-1995, went up to nearly 2 percent for the remainder of the decade, and then for 2000-2007 fell back to 1.3 percent a year (Table 2).

This trend has been paralleled in other advanced economies, the rate of per-capita growth across the Organization for Economic Cooperation and Development (OECD) falling by more than half between the 1960s and 1990s (Table 3), according to OECD statistics. World Bank data generally supports this view, and indicates a similar drop in the performance of the advanced and developing economies during this period (Tables 4 and 5).

World Bank data is less informative about global trends, but they indicate a drop in the rate of world GDP expansion, substantiated by the data compiled by the World Trade Organization (WTO). The latter shows a slowing in world GDP expansion fell-from 5.4 percent a year in the 1960s, to 4.0 percent in the 1970s, 3.2 percent in the 1980s and only 2.3 percent in the 1990s (Table 6). The drop in the rate of per capita growth is sharper still, falling from roughly 3.3 percent a year in the 1960s to 1 percent in the 1990s (Table 7).

The global picture after 2000 (or even starting in the late 1990s) is more ambiguous. According to the WTO, the years 2000-2006 have seen a 2.8 percent a year rate of growth, with per-capita improvement even more pronounced, this occurring at the rate of 1.5 percent a year (Table 8). Additionally, figures reporting twice that rate for the latter years of that period, continuing to the present, are fairly common.[8] However, it is notable that this upward swing

---

[8] It should be kept in mind that WTO numbers tend to be lower than those compiled by other institutions, such as the World Bank, and in particular the International Monetary Fund. The 2008 edition of the World Bank's *World Development Indicators* offers the following data for the latter part of this period: a 2.9 percent a year growth rate

in growth does not seem to be driven by developments in the advanced countries, but by developing nations, and that much of their economic expansion may simply reflect the surging prices of primary commodities, and in particular oil and metals, since 2002.[9] The rapid growth of Russia since the turn of the century, certainly, owes much to these factors.

Additionally, estimates of Purchasing Power Parity (PPP) figure significantly in these growth rates, and it has recently been found that this was greatly overstated in the cases of China and India, the economies of which together comprise 15-20 percent of global GDP, and have been growing at rates well above the average during this period, so that their situations alone affect the picture substantially.[10] The author has yet to encounter time series' that have been clearly adjusted to take into account these very substantial

---

for the years 1990-2000, 3 percent for 2000-2006. WB, *Indicators* 2008 (Washington D.C.: World Bank, 2008), p. 200. The International Monetary Fund's *World Economic Outlook* 2006 offers a still higher 3.4 percent a year for the 1988-1997 period, and 4.1 percent for 1998-2007. IMF, *Outlook 2006*, p. 177.

[9] World Bank, *Indicators* 2008, p. 195. This change is reflected in the indications of their shares in the figures for the total value of world merchandise exports, fuel and other mining products (and iron and steel) rising 17 percent annually for the years 2000-2006. The result was that where fuel represented just 10.2 percent of the value of world merchandise trade in 2000, it accounted for 15 percent in 2006. WTO, "World Merchandise Exports," in *International Trade Statistics 2007* (Geneva: World Trade Organization, 2008), Table II.1, p. 43. The figures for 2000 were derived from the 2001 edition of the same annual.

[10] For a discussion of this reconsideration of the estimates, see "A Less Fiery Dragon?" *The Economist*, Nov. 29, 2007. Accessed at http://www.economist.com/finance/displaystory.cfm?story_id=102 09215. A forty percent downward revision in China's 2007 GDP means a five percent downward adjustment of global GDP.

revisions. Nonetheless, even before these revelations, Alan Freeman authored a noted study which showed that, when PPP is eliminated from the picture and the current dollar figures are adjusted for inflation, the world's per capita GDP did not grow at all between 1980 and 2002, and actually shrank slightly between 1988 and the end of that period.[11]

In other words, economic growth may barely be keeping pace with the rate of population increase. The argument seems even more plausible when the deficiencies of Gross Domestic Product as a unit of measure are considered, highlighted in the common likening of GDP to "a calculating machine that adds but cannot subtract." In its estimation, no distinction is drawn between costs and benefits, or sustainable and unsustainable activities, as with the well-known example of the cancer patient who became an "economic hero" by running up a high medical bill.

In other words, GDP tends to externalize ecological and social costs, damage to long-term productivity included. Unsurprisingly, some have sought to develop alternative measures, with one notable result being the Genuine Progress Indicator (GPI),

---

[11] Alan Freeman, cited in Heikki Patomaki, *The Political Economy of Global Security: War, Future Crises and Changes in Global Governance* (New York: Routledge, 2008), p. 103. A pre-publication version of Freeman's relevant paper can be found in "Globalization: economic stagnation and divergence," Jan. 20 2008. Accessed at http://mpra.ub.uni-muenchen.de/6745/1/MPRA_paper_6745.pdf. This is all without considering the likelihood that the current figures are exaggerated by the understatement of inflation. Of course, inflation estimates were a factor in previous economic calculations, but because of the changes in the techniques used to estimate inflation (particularly innovations like "hedonics"), it seems plausible that recent figures reflect more distortion than the available estimates of earlier performance. Kevin Phillips, *Bad Money: Reckless Finance, Failed Politics and the Global Crisis of American Capitalism* (New York: Viking, 2008), pp. 80-89.

which accounts for a wide range of the aspects so often overlooked, including the consumption of capital stock (like the depreciation of infrastructure), environmental damage and resource depletion (what some term the loss of "natural" capital), unemployment, and debt.[12] Perhaps reflecting its comparatively novelty the GPI methodology has recently undergone substantial revision, and so estimates of the growth trend of recent decades have undergone comparatively substantial alteration.[13] However, it has been consistent in indicating the cessation of growth in GPI in the 1970s even as U.S. GDP has continued to expand, with the 2006 report showing virtually no per-capita increase in American prosperity between 1978 and 2004.[14]

---

[12] Clifford Cobb, Ted Halstead, and Jonathan Rowe, "If the GDP Is Up, Why Is America Down?" *Atlantic Monthly* 276.4 (Oct. 1995), pp. 59-78; and Jonathan Rowe and Judith Silverstein, "The GDP Myth: Why 'Growth' Isn't Always a Good Thing," *Washington Monthly* 31.3 (Mar. 1999), pp. 17-21.

[13] Redefining Progress, "Genuine Progress Indicator: 1998 Executive Summary." Accessed at http://www.rprogress.org/projects/gpi/updates/gpi1998_execsum.h tml#top; Redefining Progress, "Redefining Progress' Genuine Progress Indicator (GPI) Rose Slightly in 2000—Alternative Economic Measure Remains $23,947 Per Capita Below The GDP," media release, Dec. 26, 2001. Accessed at http://www.rprogress.org/media/releases/011226_gpi.html. For the most recent available estimate, which has U.S. per capita GPI at $15,000 in 2004 (roughly where it was in 1978), see Dr. John Talberth, Clifford Cobb and Noah Slattery, *The Genuine Progress Indicator 2006: A Tool for Sustainable Development* (Oakland, CA: Redefining Progress, 2007). Accessed at http://www.rprogress.org/publications/2007/GPI%202006.pdf.

[14] Indeed, this assessment suggests GDP growth has become increasingly divorced from meaningful economic progress. Talberth et. al., pp. 18-19.

Savings and Debt

Just as economic growth offers a rough picture of return on investment, savings and debt can offer a rough picture of an economy's slack. A high savings rate indicates an abundance of unused resources which can be drawn on in the event of need or opportunity, and a low level of debt indicates the same thing, while the reverse is also true. Not surprisingly, the ups and downs of both typically tie in with economic performance, periods of stagnation or contraction lowering the former.[15]

In line with the slowing of global economic growth since 1973, the indications are that this is exactly what has happened. Net savings rates have fallen across the world since the 1960s; in the case of the American private sector, from 11 percent of national income in the 1960-1979 period to 3.9 percent, with household savings dropping into the red.[16] Since the 1990s, this has even been

---

[15] "A sustained 1 percentage point increase in per capita output growth in industrial countries would over time lead to an almost 1 percent of GDP increase in the national saving rate." International Monetary Fund, World Economic Outlook, Sep. 2005, p. 98.

[16] The OECD has reported falling households savings in every member country for which data was available between 1990 and 2004, save France and Norway. No aggregate figures were published, but there were national figures. The U.S. net savings rate fell from 7 to 0.8 percent; Germany from 13.9 to 11.1 percent; Japan from 13.9 to 5.1percent. OECD, *Factbook 2005*, p. 37. For an analysis of the drop in the developed world between the 1960s and early 1990s, see Brian Bosworth, Savings and Investment in a Global Economy. Washington D.C.: Brookings, 1993. pp. 55-62. He also offered an update of his analysis, which indicated the continuation of the trend, in "United States Saving in a Global Context," Senate testimony, Apr. 6, 2006. Accessed at http://www.senate.gov/~finance/hearings/testimony/2005test/0406 06abbtest.pdf. For U.S. data, see Bosworth, testimony, "U.S. Net Savings and Investment by Sector, 1960-2005," Table 1.

the case in the countries of long high-saving Asia (China excepted).[17]

Debt, too, has substantially increased during this time frame. Public debt, particularly central government debt, has got most of the attention, and this is undeniably increasing. The proportion of gross debt to GDP more than doubled between 1974 and 2007 in the G-7 countries, from 39.3 to 79.1 percent of Gross Domestic Product.[18] Of course, gross debt may appear to overstate the problem, since governments may well amass high levels of debt while also expanding their assets, but this has generally not been the case, government assets tending to shrink instead. The result is that

---

[17] IMF, World Outlook, pp. 93-97. The observation should be qualified, however, by noting that the aging of a population places a downward pressure on national savings. IMF, p. 99. One study indicated that, in line with what economists call the "life cycle model," changes in savings rates in the developed world correlated with such demographic changes. Bosworth, Savings, pp. 62-66. The work of Burtless, however, argues that "other changes in the environment swamped whatever effects were caused by the demographic cycle" in the case of the advanced economies after the 1960s. See Gary Burtless, "Demographic Shocks and Global Factor Flows: Discussion," conference paper, 2001, p. 276. Accessed at http://www.bos.frb.org/economic/conf/conf46/conf46h2.pdf. For data on various regions, see Bosworth, testimony, "Gross Saving as Share of Regional GNI, Selected Years and Regions," Table 2b.

[18] Canadian Ministry of Finance, "G7 government net financial liabilities," Table 58. By contrast, central government debt burdens were shrinking, roughly constant or growing more slowly in the decades of faster growth prior to this period. The U.S. Federal debt notably shrank from 121.6 to 32.5 percent of GDP between 1946 and 1980, despite the regularity of modest deficits in the 1960s and 1970s. Elhefnawy, "National," pp. 127-128. For a more international view, see the 2007 *International Fiscal Reference Tables*, Tables 56 and 57. Accessed at http://www.fin.gc.ca/frt-trf/2008/frt08_9-eng.asp#57.

for the Group of Seven countries overall, the growth of net debt—gross debt minus government assets—was generally even faster after the 1970s (Table 11). In any event, the rate at which both gross and net debt grew during the first half of this decade was not much below that of the 1974-1996 period as a whole (Table 12).

Private debt has not received nearly so much attention in recent decades, and comprehensive data collection and analysis regarding that issue is (unfortunately) much more limited. However, the indications are that this too has markedly increased. In the United States alone outstanding public and private bond market debt rose from $4.5 trillion in 1985 to $22.1 trillion in 2003, from roughly 100 to over 200 percent of GDP.[19]

Mortgage and corporate debt have continued to rise rapidly since then, mortgage debt coming to nearly $13 trillion in October 2008, and corporate debt to another $7 trillion according to one report.[20] According to the Federal Reserve, consumer debt came to another $2.5 trillion at that time.[21] The result is that the total load of American *private* debt appears several times larger than the central government debt level so much more often cited.[22]

---

[19] Notably, the share of corporate and mortgage-related debt in the total figure rose from roughly 25 to 44 percent of the total figure during that time frame, another indicator of the importance of private debt accumulation. Securities Industry and Financial Markets Association, "Outstanding Level of Public & Private Bond Market Debt: 1985-2006 Q1," Apr. 1, 2003. Accessed at http://www.sifma.net/story.asp?id=323.

[20] J. Kyle Bass, Hayman Advisors, letter, Oct. 14, 2008. Accessed at http://dealbreaker.com/images/thumbs/Hayman%20Letter%20to%20Investors%20Oct%2014%20final%20version.pdf.

[21] Federal Reserve, Consumer Credit August 2008, *Federal Reserve Statistical Release*, Nov. 7 2008. Accessed at http://www.federalreserve.gov/releases/g19/Current/.

[22] This is, of course, without considering the complications arising from the internationalization of this debt, which in some cases (such

Public Finances

While not readily separable from the broader picture of national savings and debt, public finances (which entail dimensions not covered above) merit special attention. Government, more than other public or private institutions, is uniquely positioned to command societal slack in the event of exogenous shocks, or the appearance of new opportunities (as well as a bearer of the final responsibility for dealing with such exigencies). Its ability to mobilize fiscal-macroeconomic slack, which might be roughly established by considering their taxation and spending alongside their debt profile, is a way of measuring how much slack exists in a modern nation-state.

A budget surplus, for instance, can represent slack in that the state which has it possesses at least some of the means for coping with an emergency ready to hand. That is to say, for a state with relatively low levels of taxation and deficit spending, a tax raise or additional borrowing are unlikely to represent an intolerable burden, as they have more slack on which to draw (all other things being equal). By contrast, a state where these are high, or rising (particularly if this is during "normal" times) is likely to be "living beyond its means." It also has more difficulty increasing any of these to take advantage of an opportunity, or cope with an emergency, while also suggesting that public goods are becoming more expensive. The connection of public finances with more general economic performance, given government susceptibility to revenue shortfalls or surpluses, enlarged or diminished expenses in areas like

---

as the volume of foreign-held U.S. debt) may be unprecedented. Peter Drucker, Brent Schlender, "Peter Drucker Sets Us Straight," *Fortune*, Jan. 12 2004, pp. 115-118. There is also the vulnerability to a rise in interest rates that goes along with bearing a heavy debt burden to think of. See Gerald J. Swanson, Swanson, America the Broke: How the Reckless Spending of the White House and Congress are Bankrupting Our Country and Destroying Our Children's Future (New York: Currency, 2004).

unemployment relief, and rising or falling pressure to cut taxes, also help to make it a useful indicator of the level of strain on the whole system. Accordingly, this paper now turns to more closely examining the taxation and spending patterns of the advanced industrial nations.

Taxation

In keeping with "Wagner's law" that the government's share of the economy generally tends to rise, the state seems to have "grown everywhere."[23] Before World War I, tax-to-GDP ratios were at ten percent or below. Since then they have risen to 25 to 50 percent in the advanced nations, with central government revenues among the Group of Seven advanced industrial nations rising from 31.4 percent of GDP in 1970 to 38.7 percent in 2000, a level at which they have remained ever since.[24]

Christopher Hood raised a number of counterarguments to the thesis that states are pushing the limits on taxation, two of which are relevant to this discussion. (The third will be discussed later in this paper.) The first is that assuming economic growth, tax-to-GDP ratios (assuming, of course, the validity of GDP as a valid indicator of productivity) can always rise to capture increasing above-subsistence income.[25] However, subsistence should not be thought of as a fixed figure, and the cost of subsistence arguably rises as a

---

[23] World Bank, *World Development Report 1997: The State in a Changing World* (Oxford University Press, 1997), pp. 1-2.

[24] Canadian Department of Finance, "G7 general government total tax and non-tax receipts," *International Fiscal Reference Tables*, Table 54, September 2008. Accessed at http://www.fin.gc.ca/frt/2007/frt07_9e.html#54.

[25] Christopher Hood, "The Tax State in the Information Age," in T.V. Paul, John A. Hall and G. John Ikenberry, eds., *The Nation-State in Question* (Princeton, N.J.: Princeton University, 2003), p. 216.

society develops. Even food provision or basic sanitation is a different matter for a densely populated industrial country than a smaller, more dispersed agrarian population.

Hood's second counterargument is that the maximum tax level previously attained ought not to be confused with the practical limits of such capability. In an emergency a government could always increase taxes and possibly extract more revenue for a time. Still, higher taxes do not always mean a government will successfully raise more money, as the problems of subsistence and evasion demonstrate. A considerable body of economic theory also discusses the tendency of governments to maximize their revenue, a particularly well-known example of which is Mancur Olson's "stationary bandit" model of government. There is thus reason to believe that actual tax levels bear some relationship to the limits of such taxation, at least over the long run.

Additionally, tax levels do not always return to pre-crisis levels after a crisis ends, so that peacetime tax levels can reflect a not irrelevant previous "crisis maximum," as the case of the U.S. before, during and after World War II demonstrates. At the beginning of World War II, central government tax revenue was less than seven percent of GDP in the U.S.. During the war it went up to twenty percent. After the war it fell from this high, but only to about fourteen percent—twice as high as it was before the war. Since then they continued to increase, until in the 1990s it was back at 1944 levels.[26]

Moreover, there is no escaping the question of public tolerance for taxation, which always generates a measure of resistance, avoidance, and evasion, greater when seen as excessive or illegitimate, and which can take legal (like the more intensive exploitation of loopholes, "investment strikes," and capital flight) as well as illegal forms. Processing costs, and enforcement costs, too,

---

[26] Nader Elhefnawy, "National Mobilization: An Option in Future Conflicts?" *Parameters* 34.3 (Autumn 2004), pp. 127-130.

must be taken into account on the credits side of the balance sheet, and these go up in exactly that situation.[27] As the furor over the 1988 British poll tax demonstrated, the reaction to even relatively small increases can be prohibitive, and the failure of many of the major economies to raise taxes despite considerable pressure to do so in recent years (in the U.S. because of the multi-trillion dollar costs of the War on Terror, in Japan because of exploding government debt in the 1990s and 2000s, in France and Germany because of the discipline required by the European Union's Stability and Growth Pact) is indicative of their approaching the political (though not necessarily economic) limits on their ability to raise revenue.

Spending

As might be expected given rising government debt, spending rose at an even swifter pace than taxation in the post-war era, from 32.1 percent of GDP in the G-7 nations in 1970 to a peak of 42.2 percent in 1993.[28] Despite post-Cold War military drawdowns; the scaling back of welfare states; major reductions in public spending on infrastructure and research and development; and the savings that privatizing and decentralizing government services were supposed to generate; they actually achieved only very limited reductions.[29] The lowest point they attained after this was 38.7

---

[27] It was recently estimated that illegal evasion deprives the U.S. Treasury of $300 billion a year. Robert J. Samuelson, "The Price of Democracy," *Newsweek*, May 17, 2004.

[28] Canadian Ministry of Finance, "G7 government net outlays," Table 55.

[29] OECD, "Education at a Glance-OECD Indicators 1998," November 23, 1998, http://www1.oecd.org/media/publish/pb98-42a.htm. Barry Bosworth, "Prospects for Savings and Investment in Industrial Countries," *Brookings Discussion Papers* 113 (Washington D.C.: Brookings, 1995). OECD, *Economic Outlook* 69 (June 2001), p. 182. The modest success in achieving reductions is reflective of the large and rising share of mandatory spending in

percent of GDP in 2000 (in part because GDP had been growing somewhat more rapidly in the late 1990s in the advanced Western nations), but since 2002 the figure has not dropped below the 40 percent level.

The same trend is evident in the swelling of central government budget deficits, from an average of 1.2 percent of GDP in the early 1970s to 4 percent in the 1980s (Table 9), pushing the level the IMF has identified as the maximum safe one. In the early 1990s, the average deficit ran at an even higher 4.3 percent, but dropped with the boom in the later part of the decade, many countries actually running surpluses at this time, high-spending Japan the notable exception (Table 10). With the waning of that boom, however, deficit spending returned to the levels of the early '90s, the average deficit for the years 2002-2005 coming to 4.2 percent of Gross Domestic Product (Table 10).[30]

In short, it seems to be all they can do to hold down the growth of deficit spending. And this is all without considering the likely understatement of those deficits, government accounts long being notoriously deceptive. In the case of the U.S., one observer noted that the official $248 billion Federal deficit of 2006 would actually come to $1.3 trillion were "corporate-style accounting" used.[31]

---

national budgets (like debt service). IMF, *World Economic Outlook*, May 2000, p. 173.

[30] The data indicates an improvement in the fiscal picture after 2005, again, correlating with the reported acceleration of growth in the same time frame.

[31] Dennis Cauchon, "Taxpayers on the Hook for $59 trillion," *USA Today*, May 28, 2007. Accessed at http://www.usatoday.com/news/washington/2007-05-28-federal-budget_N.htm. Dennis Cauchon, "Taxpayers on the Hook for $59 trillion," *USA Today*, May 28, 2007. Accessed at http://www.usatoday.com/news/washington/2007-05-28-federal-budget_N.htm.

Assessing the Evidence, Considering the Consequences and Finding Explanations

Since the 1970s there has been a clear trend toward falling, stagnating and by some measures, even negative rates of economic growth; falling saving rates; rising debt, both public and private; and strained public finances, with budget cuts and tax raises both increasingly difficult, compared with the case in previous decades. The result is a vicious cycle that keeps those debts growing, while the weight of these debt burdens contributes to continued economic stagnation (not least, by tying the hands of government with regard to ameliorative action).

In short, the signs indicate that the fiscal-macroeconomic slack of the world's major states, and the international system overall, are decreasing as a proportion of their overall (and more slowly growing) resources, and their recent behavior reflects this, particularly the reticence about launching major new initiatives in recent decades (and indeed, a retreat from responsibility in at least some areas) that gave rise to much talk of "the decline of the state" (less fashionable than a few years ago, though the fundamentals of the discourse have changed little). It also bodes poorly for the likelihood of today's states taking preventive approaches to problems or to handle them when they are small, before they become impossible to ignore but much more costly to deal with (for example, environmental problems like global warming).

Examining the data, it becomes apparent that the 1970s represent a turning point, economic growth rates dropping sharply after that time, a development strongly related to the rapid rise of debt-to-GDP ratios, that also occurred during those years.[32] Of course, it is the case that the exceptional growth of the 1950s and 1960s was tied to the unique production efforts of the United States

---

[32] The per capita global economic growth, extrapolated from the same WTO data series noted above, came to roughly 3 percent a year for the years 1950-1973. After 1973 it has been in the area of 1.3 percent a year, less than half as much.

and other belligerents, high levels of Cold War discretionary spending and the subsequent rebuilding of Europe and Asia. However, these boosts to the world economy were unrepeatable, and entailed their own strains, which led to other, disruptive changes, among them the abandonment of the Bretton Woods monetary system; and the exploding resource consumption that helped precipitate the "energy crisis" of the 1970s.

Nonetheless, these have generally not been viewed as fully accounting for the change, and numerous explanations above and beyond these enjoy some currency. One oft-made observation among critics of the trend is that this pattern coincided with a shift in economic policies toward neoliberalism, making possible economic globalization in the form in which we now know it (with its undeniable, massive increase of the complexity of economic life). From there many have gone on to suggest that neoliberal policies have simply been inferior to those characterizing the more regulated, "mixed" economies of mid-century at "delivering the goods."[33]

The correlation is undeniable, but the establishment of causality is more challenging. Historically, the literature has focused on the national consequences of national policies, rather than more global studies, especially when the question of narrowly economic performance is considered.[34] Nonetheless, enough work has been

---

[33] John Ralston Saul, *The Collapse of Globalism: and the Reinvention of the World* (Woodstock: Overlook Press, 2005); Gerald Epstein, ed., *Financialization and the World Economy* (Cheltenham, UK: Edward Elger, 2005). Also see Paul Bairoch, *Economics and World History: Myths and Paradoxes* (Chicago: University of Chicago Press, 1995), pp. 3-55; Patomaki, who has connected the movement to and from free trade with the upswings and downswings of economic long waves, in Patomaki, pp. 100-123.

[34] Heikki Patomaki noted that "relatively few economists have actually studied long-term global trends in any systematic fashion." Patomaki, p. 102.

done in this and related areas for these critiques to at least point to some plausible connections between these policies, and the economic trends of the last three decades.

Wage-Productivity Gaps

Economist Ravi Batra has pointed to the expansion of wage-productivity gaps as a major obstacle for economic growth. The reason is that the drop in wages suppresses consumption, which can only be sustained by the accumulation of debt. At the same time, the weakness of consumption discourages investment in expanded production, and encourages its diversion into speculative channels——the buying and selling of assets rather than goods and services——which in turn negatively impacts financial stability and growth (the consequences of which Batra finds in the weakened economic performance of many advanced economies, the U.S. in particular).[35] Neoliberalism, by withdrawing government support for labor, weakening controls on investment flows (and with it, the mobility of capital), and intensifying international competition, has clearly contributed to such a situation, epitomized in what some have taken to calling "the China price."[36] It has also been argued that low wages discourage labor-saving, productivity-enhancing investments ("the low-wage trap"), undermining the growth trend yet again.

"Short-Termism"

---

[35] See Ravi Batra, *Greenspan's Fraud* (New York: Palgrave Macmillan, 2005), pp. 142-167. The expansion of the financial sector relative to the rest of the economy in the U.S. has been noted by many critics with alarm. Finance and insurance went from comprising 11 percent of U.S. GDP in 1987 to 14 percent in 1986; real estate from 14 percent to 16 percent during the same time frame. For a critique of the trend, see Phillips, *Bad Money*, pp. 29-119.

[36] Alexandra Harney, *The China Price: The True Cost of Chinese Competitive Advantage* (New York: Penguin, 2008).

The intensified competition and financialization discussed above have also contributed to a more general "short-termism," by which is meant the short time horizon of company managers prioritizing a short-term outlook over a long-term one, a tendency commonly connected with the increased influence that a less constrained financial sector has attained over non-financial corporations (NFCs). And indeed, a small but growing academic literature on the subject now exists.[37] A widely noted addition to that literature in 2005 confirmed the tendency of corporate executives to favor "smooth earnings" and short-term stock prices over value, and a readiness to achieve this desired result not only by way of accounting, but actions sacrificing research and development, maintenance, and other such essentials.[38] Economist James Crotty has also made a compelling case that financialization has led to an emphasis on sustaining stock prices and fighting hostile takeovers (dependent on debt-financed stock buys and special dividends) at the expense of capital accumulation and innovation, and with increasing indebtedness as a result (as well as continuous cost-cutting pressures of the kind discussed by Batra, with their effects).[39]

---

[37] For a discussion of this, see Angela Black and Patricia Fraser, "Stock market short-termism-an international perspective," *Journal of Multinational Financial Management* 12.2 (April 2002), pp. 135-158.

[38] The study found that 78 percent would sacrifice value for smooth earnings, that 80 percent would sacrifice R & D and maintenance to achieve this end, and that 55 percent were willing to delay a project at the expense of value for the same purposes. John R. Graham, Campbell R. Harvey, and Shivaram Rajgopal, "The Economic Implications of Corporate Financial Reporting," *Journal of Accounting and Economics* 40 (2005), pp. 3–73.

[39] James Crotty, "The Neoliberal Paradox: The Impact of Destructive Product Market Competition and Impatient Finance on Nonfinancial Corporations in the Neoliberal Era," Policy Economic Research Institute, Research Brief (Jul. 2003); Crotty, "The Neoliberal Paradox: The Impact of Destructive Product Market

It may also be the case that business responds in such a situation by deploying the resources that go to areas like R & D in different ways, one analyst arguing that the energy sector has reacted to the competitive pressures it faces by emphasizing "conservative innovations able to pay off in the short term" rather than "system-shattering" research.[40]

Competition and 'Modern' Financial Markets on Nonfinancial Corporations in the Neoliberal Era," in Epstein, ed., *Financialization*, pp. 77-107. It may also be that leanness itself poorly positions a company for expansion, recent research indicating that slack in its capacity may be essential for business growth at the entrepreneurial level as well. See Theresa M. Welbourne, Heidi M. Neck, G. Dale Meyer, "Human Resource Slack and Venture Growth," conference paper. Accessed at http://www.babson.edu/entrep/fer/papers99/XXII/XXII_A/XXII_A .html.

[40] For the case of the energy industry, see Marshall Goldberg, "Federal Energy Subsidies: Not All Technologies Are Created Equal," *Renewable Energy Policy Project*, Research Report, July 2000, p. 2. This area is particularly relevant, because where some sectors of technological R & D may be offering diminishing returns to investment, this appears to be one where chronic underinvestment has been the norm. See Robert M. Margolis and Daniel M. Kammen, "Underinvestment: The Energy Technology and R & D Policy Challenge," *Science* 285 (Jul. 1999), pp. 690-692; Margolis and Kammen, "Energy R & D Innovation: Challenges and Opportunities for Technology and Climate Policy," in Stephen Schneider, Armin Rosencranz, and John-O Niles, eds., *A Reader in Climate Change Policy* (Washington D.C.: Island Press, 2001). More broadly, such a tendency may at least partially account for the diminishing marginal returns on technological investment some observers have identified in recent decades, with information technology discussed as a lone exception. Michael O'Hanlon, *Technological Change and the Future of Warfare* (Washington D.C.: Brookings Institution Press, 2000), p. 194; W. Brian Arthur, "Increasing Returns and the New World of Business," *Harvard Business Review*, 74.4 (Jul.-Aug.

Long-range growth and innovation aside, the drive "toward leaner operations and ever-shorter time horizons" comes at the expense of the robustness and reliability of a business's operations, and it is at least plausible that this imposes other costs on the larger economy in which it operates, comparatively invisible because they are externalized from the business's own balance sheet.[41] Utility companies offer a useful example. In the U.S. following deregulation, electricity companies pursued a gamut of cost-cutting measures, some of these at the price of grid reliability. While the issue has been little studied at the macroeconomic level, there is evidence that the damage done to the U.S. economy as a whole in this way may far exceed any savings it gains at that level.[42]

1996), pp. 100-109. However, Robert J. Gordon has noted the limits of the contributions computers and the Internet have made to the global economy, and Roland Spant has written about the macroeconomic effects of the rapid depreciation of IT. Robert J. Gordon, "Does the 'New Economy' Measure up to the Great Inventions of the Past?" *Journal of Economic Perspectives* 14.4 (Fall 2000), pp. 49-74; Roland Spant, "Why Net Domestic Product should replace Gross Domestic Product as a Measure of Economic Growth," *International Productivity Monitor* 7 (Fall 2003), pp. 39-43. Accessed at http://www.csls.ca/ipm/7/spant-e.pdf. Part of the problem may also lie in poor decision-making at the adoption end of the process as well. Rochlin, *Trapped*, pp. 29-34.

[41] Nader Elhefnawy, "Societal Complexity," p. 166.

[42] One assessment is that grid unreliability cost the U.S. economy $120 billion in 2001 alone. George F. McClure, "Electric Power Transmission Reliability Not Keeping Pace with Conservation Efforts," *Today's Engineer Online*, Feb. 2005. Accessed at http://www.todaysengineer.org/2005/Feb/reliability.asp. For an assessment of the economic costs of a single recent U.S. blackout (the August 2003 blackout in the northeastern United States), see Electricity Consumers Resource Council, "The Economic Effects of the August 2003 Blackout," Feb. 9, 2004. Accessed at

Ecological Damage and Resource Depletion

Finally, it is arguable that the new international business environment has contributed to the failure to address the depletion and pollution of natural resources by restraining government policy in this area and helping "reward" those states most willing to absorb such damage with growth (again, as in the case of China). While the tendency has been to write in terms of a trade-off between economic growth and ecology, the reality is that damage to the latter must inevitably diminish the former.

Indeed, at a global level the sustenance of growth through increased resource exploitation appears to have broached its limits. An oft-cited estimate by the World Wildlife Fund in 1999 was that the world economy is now consuming resources equivalent to those of 1.2 Earth "equivalents," a figure that had risen to 1.4 Earths by 2008, and is on track to reach the level of two Earth equivalents by the mid-2030s.[43]

While GDP does not register such costs in a comprehensive way, it nonetheless registers some of the effects in slower or negative growth, and even though the global picture of the economic impact of these patterns is sketchy, in the 1990s the Asian Development Bank estimated that the economic costs of environmental degradation ranged from 1-9 percent of a country's gross economic product.[44] According to that analysis, China alone

---

http://www.elcon.org/Documents/EconomicImpactsOfAugust2003 Blackout.pdf.

[43] Worldwatch Institute, ed., *Vital Signs, 2003: The Trends That Are Shaping Our Future* (New York: W.W. Norton & Co., 2003), pp. 44-45. Also see Rob Costanza, "Natural Capital, Ecosystem Services," *Nature*(May 1997), pp. 253-254. For the more recent data, see the World Wildlife Fund Living Planet Report 2008, http://assets.panda.org/downloads/living_planet_report_2008.pdf.

[44] One estimate has these at eight percent of GDP in some Asian nations. S. Tahir Qadri, ed., *Asian Environmental Outlook 2001* (Manila, Philippines: Asian Development Bank, 2001), p. 11.

suffered an 8 percent loss in the form of damage to its agriculture, production and natural resources from air and water pollution.

Neoliberalism and Public Finances

In addition to the broad economic consequences sketched above, it is worth noting that neoliberal globalization has also impacted public finances in more direct ways. Besides the matters of economic growth always creating potential additional resources; and the distance between current tax levels and the theoretical limits of capability; Christopher Hood raises the question of specific options with regard to tax collection. As he acknowledges, neoliberal globalization has not only restricted the scope for tariffs (once an important revenue source for many states), but taxes on capital, marginal income and corporate taxes.[45] While arguments have often been advanced that states can successfully reject the neoliberal path, globalization is more likely to harm than help such efforts.[46]

The result has been more regressive taxation, not only in the downward revision of many of these rates, but a greater dependence on "salary taxes," which affect lower- and middle-income taxpayers most, and increasingly, flat taxes well.[47] Given widening inequality, soft job markets and wages that may be stagnant or even falling in their actual purchasing power (with all the consequences this has for consumption, and growth), this increasingly confines taxation to a

---

[45] Hood, p. 217. Not surprisingly, while polls in democratic countries indicate a general sentiment that corporations and the wealthy are under-taxed, the taxes of these groups have generally been lowered rather than raised. Ibid., p. 218.

[46] Rudra Sil, "Globalization, The State and Industrial Relations: Common Challenges, Divergent Transitions," in *The Nation-State in Question*, p. 285.

[47] Allan Sloan, "Why Your Tax Cut Doesn't Add Up," *Newsweek*, Apr. 12, 2004, pp. 41-46. Social Security is not levied on income above a specified, annually adjusted level-$94,200 in 2006.

smaller part of the overall tax base, and makes simple tax-to-GDP ratios (already problematic given GDP's failings as a measure of wealth) an underestimation of the strain on the system.[48] Such situations consequently translate into greater difficulty increasing revenue, even during acknowledged national emergencies.[49]

Conclusions

There are at least the rudiments for making the case that the policies identified with neoliberal globalization (the reduction of labor protections, deregulated financial flows, etc.) are, by way of their impacts on consumption and investment, closely connected with the current tendency toward maladaptive investments in complexity (in their delivering slowing economic growth), and along with it, the (relative) erosion of fiscal-macroeconomic slack that recent decades have witnessed (as indicated by falling savings, the growth of public and private debt, and the tightening of government finances). Tentative as any argument along these lines necessarily is at this point, at the very least it can suggest future directions for research, and in turn, possible paths toward ameliorating the problems with which policy-makers have grappled with such clear lack of success since the 1970s.

---

[48] It cannot be assumed that elevated incomes in the upper quintiles during periods of skewed income distribution will compensate either in the area of savings or overall tax collection, as promised by proponents of Federal tax cuts in the U.S. in the 1980s. The result was instead the dramatic increase in the national debt during those years. Charles Kindleberger, *World Economic Primacy: 1500-1990* (Oxford University Press, 1996), p. 179.

[49] Ibid., p. 100. The point is demonstrated by the frequency with which such situations figure in portraits of societal collapse. For more on that tendency, see Carlo Cipolla, ed., *The Economic Decline of Empires*(London: Meuthen, 1970).

TABLES

Presented below are the paper's associated tables, of which there are five sets in all covering U.S. Economic Performance, 1950-2007; Comparative Economic Growth Rates, 1960-2004; World Economic Performance, 1950-2006; Central Government Deficits Relative to GDP in the G-7 Countries, 1970-2007; and Central Government Debt Growth Relative to GDP in the G-7 Countries; along with the sources from which the data was derived. All figures are given as percentages.

U.S. Economic Performance, 1950-2007

Table 1. Annual (%) Rate of Real Growth in U.S. Gross Domestic Product, 1950-2007 (By Decade)

Period	Total	Per Capita
1950-1960	3.8	2
1960-1970	4.1	2.7
1970-1980	2.3	1.3
1980-1990	2.7	1.8
1990-2000	2.5	1.2
2000-2007	2.3	1.3

Table 2. Annual (%) Rate of Real Growth in U.S. Gross Domestic Product, 1950-2007 (Selected Periods)

Period	Total	Per Capita
1950-1973	4.2	2.7
1973-1995	2	1
1995-2000	3.2	1.9
2000-2007	2.3	1.3
1973-2000	2.2	1.2
1973-2007	2.2	1.3
1995-2007	2.6	1.6

Source: Calculated using GDP data (current dollars, annual series) from Bureau of Economic Analysis, "Gross Domestic Product," Frequently Requested NIPA Tables, Interactive Access to National Income and Product Accounts Tables, Table 1.1.5; the Bureau of Labor Statistics inflation calculator; and population data from the U.S. Census Bureau International Data Base (U.S. country summary, midyear population estimates).

Comparative Economic Growth Rates, 1960-2004

Table 3. Annual (%) Rate of Real Growth in the Gross Domestic Product of the Organization for Economic Cooperation and Development Member States, 1960-2004 (Selected Periods)

Period	Total	Per Capita
1960-1973	4.9	3.7
1970-1973	5.1	3.9
1973-1979	3	2
1979-1989	2.8	2
1989-2000	2.6	1.8
1992-2000	2.5	N/A
2000-2004	2.1	N/A
1973-1989	2.9	2
1973-2000	2.7	1.9

Source: OECD, "Real Gross Domestic Product," Historical Statistics: 1960-1997 (OECD, 1999), Table 3.2, p. 50, and "Real GDP Per Capita," Table 3.2, p. 50; "Real Gross Domestic Product," Historical Statistics: 1970-2000 (OECD, 2001), Table 3.1, p. 48, and "Real GDP Per Capita", Table 3.2, p. 48. Figures for 1992-2002 calculated from OECD Health Data 2004, 1st ed., cited in OECD news release, Jun. 3 2004, Table 1, p. 1; data for 2001-2004 from OECD Factbook 2005 (OECD, 2005), p. 31.

Table 4. Annual (%) Rate of Real Growth in the Gross Domestic Product of Advanced and Developing Countries, 1960-2000 (By Decade)

Period	Advanced	Developing
1960-1970	5.4	5.8
1970-1980	3.8	5.1
1980-1990	3.1	2.6
1990-2000	2.5	3.5

Table 5. Annual (%) Rate of Real Growth in the Per-Capita Gross Domestic Product of Advanced and Developing Countries, 1960-2000 (By Decade)

Period	Advanced	Developing
1960-1970	4.2	3.6
1970-1980	2.6	2.9
1980-1990	2.5	0.7
1990-2000	1.8	1.8

Source: World Bank, World Development Indicators 2004, cited in World Bank, "Growth in Developed and Developing Countries," in Economic Growth in the 1990s (Washington D.C.: World Bank, 2005), Table 3.1, p. 62.

World Economic Performance, 1950-2006

Table 6. Annual (%) Rate of Real Growth in Gross World Product,
1950-2006 (By Decade)

Period	WTO Data	World Bank Data
1950-1960	4.6	N/A
1960-1970	5.4	N/A
1970-1980	4	3.6
1980-1990	3.2	3.3
1990-2000	2.3	2.9
2000-2006	2.8	3

Table 7. Annual (%) Rate of Real Growth in Per Capita Gross
World Product, 1950-2006 (By Decade)

Period	WTO Data	World Bank Data
1950-1960	2.5	N/A
1960-1970	3.3	N/A
1970-1980	2.1	1.7
1980-1990	1.4	1.5
1990-2000	1	1.4
2000-2006	1.5	1.6

Source: WTO GDP data calculated from World Trade Organization,
"World merchandise exports, production and gross domestic
product, 1950-2006," International Trade Statistics 2007 (Geneva:
World Trade Organization, 2007), Table A1, p. 169. World Bank
GDP growth figures compiled from World Bank, "Gross Domestic
Product," World Tables, 1993 ed. (Washington D.C.: World Bank,
1993), Table 6, p. 24; Ibid., "Gross Domestic Product," World
Tables, 1995 ed. (Washington D.C.: World Bank, 1995), Table 6,
pp. 24-25; Ibid., "Growth of Output," World Development

Indicators 2004 (Washington D.C.: World Bank, 2004), Table 4.1, p. 184; Ibid., "Growth of Output," World Development Indicators 2008 (Washington D.C.: World Bank, 2008), Table 4.1, p. 200. Population data from U.S. Census Bureau, International Data Base, "Total Midyear Population for the World: 1950-2050."

Table 8. Annual (%) Rate of Real Growth in Total and Per Capita Gross World Product, 1950-2006 (Selected Periods)

Period	Total	Per Capita
1950-1973	5	3
1973-1995	2.9	1.2
1995-2000	3.1	1.7
2000-2006	2.8	1.5
1973-2000	2.9	1.3
1973-2006	2.9	1.3
1995-2006	2.9	1.8

Source: Calculated from WTO, "World merchandise exports, production and gross domestic product, 1950-2006"; and U.S. Census Bureau, International Data Base, "Total Midyear Population for the World: 1950-2050."

Central Government Deficits Relative to GDP in the G-7 Countries, 1970-2007

Table 9. Average Annual (%) Budget Deficit in the G-7 Countries, 1970-2007 (By Decade)

Period	Average Deficit
1970-1980	2.3
1980-1990	4
1990-2000	3.1
2000-2007	2.9

Table 10. Average Annual (%) Budget Deficit in the G-7
Countries, 1970-2007 (Selected Periods)

Period	Average Deficit
1970-1974	1.2
1975-1980	3.3
1980-1990	4
1991-1996	4.3
1997-2001	1.2
2002-2005	4.2
2006-2007	2.3
1975-2006	3.8
1975-2007	3.5
1997-2007	2.5

Source: Calculated from Canadian Ministry of Finance,
"International Fiscal Comparisons," Fiscal Reference Tables, Sep.
29, 2008. Accessed at
http://www.fin.gc.ca/frt/2008/frt08_9e.html#54.

**Central Government Debt Growth Relative to GDP in the G-7
Countries**

Table 11. Annual (%) Rate of Growth of Central Government Debt
in the G-7 Countries (By Decade)

Period	Net Debt	Gross Debt
1970-1980	-0.3	0.8
1980-1990	4.6	2.5
1990-2000	1.8	1.8
2000-2007	2.1	1.6

Table 12. Annual (%) Rate of Growth of Central Government Debt
in the G-7 Countries (Selected Periods)

Period	Net Debt	Gross Debt
1970-1974	-4.9	-2.3
1974-1980	2.7	2.8
1980-1990	4.6	2.5
1974-1996	4.2	2.9
1990-1996	5	4.9
1996-2000	-2.9	-1
2000-2005	3.5	2.7
2000-2007	2.1	1.6

Source: Calculated from Canadian Ministry of Finance, "International Fiscal Comparisons," Fiscal Reference Tables, Sep. 29, 2008. Accessed at http://www.fin.gc.ca/frt/2008/frt08_9e.html#54.

ABOUT THE AUTHOR

Nader Elhefnawy has degrees in International Relations and Literature from Florida International University and the University of Miami. He has published on the subjects of complexity, economics and security in the journals *International Security*, *Survival* and *Parameters*, and more recently authored the historical study, *Geography, Technology and the Flux of Opportunity: The Rise and Decline of British Economic Power*. Nader Elhefnawy can be found online at his blog, *Raritania*.